D1507139

SNOWSHOEING
THROUGH SEWERS

Other Works by Michael Aaron Rockland

NONFICTION

Sarmiento's Travels in the United States in 1847 (1970)

*America in the Fifties and Sixties: Julian Marias
on the United States* (editor) (1972)

The American Jewish Experience in Literature (1975)

Homes on Wheels (1980)

Looking for America on the New Jersey Turnpike
(coauthored with Angus Kress Gillespie) (1989)

FICTION

A Bliss Case (1989)

SCREENPLAY

Three Days on Big City Waters
(coauthored with Charles Woolfolk) (1974)

SNOWSHOEING THROUGH SEWERS

Adventures in New York City, New Jersey, and Philadelphia

MICHAEL AARON ROCKLAND

RUTGERS UNIVERSITY PRESS • NEW BRUNSWICK, NEW JERSEY

Some of these stories had earlier incarnations in various magazines and journals. The author wishes to thank the editors of *New Jersey Monthly, Philadelphia Magazine, Explorer's Journal, Adventure Travel,* and *New Jersey Outdoors* for their kind permission to adapt the stories and recast them in their present form. The story "A Tale of Two Canals" is adapted, in part, from a lecture delivered at the Macculloch Hall Museum's symposium on the Morris Canal at Drew University in October 1991.

Library of Congress Cataloging-in-Publication Data

Rockland, Michael Aaron.
    Snowshoeing through sewers : adventures in New York City, New
Jersey, and Philadelphia / Michael Aaron Rockland.
       p. cm.
    ISBN 0-8135-2115-7 :
    1. New Jersey—Description and travel. 2. New York (N.Y.)—
Description and travel. 3. Philadelphia, (Pa.)—Description and
travel. I. Title.
F140.R63 1994
917.4—dc20   94-10145
                                                                         CIP

British Cataloging-in-Publication information available

*The Buddha, the Godhead, resides quite as comfortably
in the circuits of a digital computer or the gears of
a cycle transmission as he does at the top of a mountain
or in the petals of a flower.*

Robert M. Pirsig,
Zen and the Art of Motorcycle Maintenance

*For my urban adventure comrades: Joe Chapel,
Angus Gillespie, Jack Roberts, Charlie Woolfolk,
and, especially, Phil Herbert.*

*And for Barbara Rubin and Larry Rockland, who shared
my earliest urban adventures; and David Rockland,
Jeffrey Rockland, and Keren Rockland McGinity, who
shared later ones.*

Contents

SNOWSHOEING
THROUGH SEWERS

Introduction

[Let us] speculate a bit about the beer can by the highway, which at night picks up the beams from your car's headlights and glows like a panther's eye.

JOHN KOUWENHOVEN, *BEER CAN BY THE HIGHWAY*

Although I didn't know it at the time, the idea for this book came to me years ago at a place in New Jersey just off Interstate 287, a highway that wends its way along the western fringe of the megalopolis. The place on 287 was nothing special; I doubt I could find it again. I was on my way to work and stopped there to . . . well, just because I wanted to stop. Perhaps I was tired of being responsible; maybe I needed a minivacation.

All my life I had driven along highways and fantasized stopping and running up the nearest hill—straight up it, even if that meant passing through backyards or over fences or across farmers' fields to get there. It always seemed a shame to pass those hills without sampling even one of them.

In less ambitious moments, when a hill seemed too daunting, I fantasized stopping anywhere, anywhere at all, and just wandering into the woods by the side of the road. What evidence of roadside dramas might I find? A bit of frayed tire, a single shoe, a rotting tennis ball? And if there was no sign of man, would I not still have made a kind of pilgrimage to the trees and vines and berry bushes, or to the tiny swamps created by the highway's interference, which flourish unnoticed as we crash by in our motorized rooms?

But there were always too many hills and countless miles of roadside to choose among; and, of course, I was always on my way somewhere and, like any good citizen, locked into the idea of getting there as soon as possible. Maybe I was afraid that if I stopped and headed aimlessly off the road I would never come back.

But that day on Interstate 287 I just did it. Careful not to be too abrupt, what with all those eighteen-wheelers glowering down at me as they clanked and thumped over the potholes and tar joints, I eased my car off the road and onto the grass.

The grass and weeds, which until recently had luxuriated, now were beginning to tire, to mat down. Off to the right was a rocky hillside with sumacs already coloring in the early autumn air. I decided to climb the hill, though I felt a little foolish. What if the state police stopped and demanded to know what I was doing? Who owns the side of the road anyway?

But it felt good on top of that hill. It reminded me of when I was a boy and played king of the mountain on a similar hill in the park. All the years between that earlier place and this one suddenly telescoped; I felt energized, full of an unexplained joy. Looking down on the traffic racing by, and over the far hills to where the New Jersey flats began, I felt as if I possessed the landscape, as if I was once again king of the mountain.

I decided to explore along the ridge of the hill. The fact that I surely would be late for work seemed unimportant when compared with possibly discovering when last a human being had been up on that hill. Might a Leni-Lenape Indian have stood where I was three hundred years ago? Surely a member of the crew who built the highway had been on this spot. The crew might even have created the hill from dirt and rocks they piled up when flattening the roadbed.

Whatever, someone had been up there in recent history, for shining forth from the darkness under a grove of pine trees was a beer can. As I lifted it out of the needles, the rusted bottom crumbled and fell to the ground.

On another day that discarded can might have made me angry. But this can was well on its way to becoming soil. Besides, there is still enough of the boy in me to find charm in junk, to enjoy the town dump or an abandoned railroad yard as much as any park or Rembrandt or pharaoh's tomb. Life isn't neat, and there is a certain beauty in the haphazard landscape. There are worse things in life than litter.

The sun had warmed the pines, and their aroma enveloped me; for once my inner life and sense of place seemed one and the same. I stretched out on the pine needles thinking I might lie there forever.

I could hear the trucks roaring below. Just as loudly, the year's last cicadas droned in the trees above me. Each sound seemed incomplete without the other. I felt suspended between two worlds, at the very nexus of nature and the built environment. Just lying there, I was engaged in a particular kind of adventure, exploring a new frontier.

That frontier is where this book takes place. Always before, my adventures had been on the rock-strewn trails of rugged peaks or along white-water rivers. But now, as I thought of those adventures, I recalled that my biggest outdoor thrills had occurred not in the desolate wilds but when, in thick woods, I discovered a collapsing stone wall; when, in the city, I espied an ailanthus, the tree of heaven, emerging from a crack in the sidewalk. It was the sudden meeting of man's works and nature, whether in the wilderness or the city, that excited me.

Before, like other Americans, I had thought of adventure as escape, as what you experienced away from people. Like Daniel Boone I had always headed out. Like Henry David Thoreau I had dreamed of building a shack on a solitary pond and believed that true adventure requires being "ready to leave father and mother, and brother and sister, and wife and child and friends, and never see them again."

But lying there in the pines above Interstate 287, I felt my attachments with greater poignancy than ever. The events that customarily precipitate American adventures had not occurred. My wife had not left me. I had not received a pink slip with my paycheck. A husky-voiced caller had not phoned to say, "Flee, all is discovered."

Even if such unfortunate events had transpired, where was there to escape to anymore? The beer can on that hillside was a reminder that there is already litter on Everest and that the last little rain forest cannibal, with bone-pierced nose and poison-dart blowpipe, has starred in a documentary. Besides, I couldn't head for the Himalayas or the jungle. I had a mortgage; I had children.

Still, I craved adventure, wanted to be, in some measure, the hero of my own life. Chalk it up to midlife crisis if you want. Tell me that mature men shouldn't need this kind of validation. Maybe so. But when a man knows for sure that he will never, ever, equal the exploits of Hillary or Chichester or Peary or Byrd, may he not be forgiven for casting about for something else? All I knew was that I powerfully wanted to do things no one had done before, to explore some unknown terrain.

I began to think: *perhaps I could adventure not where no one has been but where no one wishes to go.*

If I couldn't, like Thor Heyerdahl, cross the Pacific on a balsa log raft, perhaps I could hike across traffic-clogged cities or bike the continuous parking lots of wall-to-wall suburban malls or canoe the sinister waterways that seep through rusting industrial sites. These are often scenes of horror, but they may also have a peculiar beauty. At night, with the lights and flaring gas of the refineries at their brightest, the industrial badlands of New Jersey are as beautiful in their way as the eroded Badlands of South Dakota.

Thoreau explored an unspoiled Merrimack River. The Merrimack today is filthy, but does that make it any the less interesting to the true adventurer? Adventure need not be confined to pleasant landscapes. Our most interesting "rivers" today might even be the man-made ones flowing underground in sewers—however much we choose not to know anything about them and make sure to direct our feet away from where they flow.

To put it another way: in the late twentieth century, a weed- and trash-filled city lot or even a hillside above an interstate may be a better place than the wilderness to contemplate one's relationship to nature. For these are now the everyday scenes of our lives, and if we crave adventure, then why not adventure here, through the built environment, through our own habitat? My home is as much a part of nature as any beaver's or wasp's.

Enough of escape! "Go west, young man" doesn't cut it for me anymore, nor, I suspect, for America. My country and I are no longer young, and the West no longer embodies our dreams. And half of us are women. "Go east, middle-aged America" might be a better slogan—not literally east but back into civilization, back into community.

This, then, is a book that seeks to redefine adventure in contemporary terms. During the half-dozen years since that hillside episode along Interstate 287, on weekends and during vacation periods, I have traversed the very heart of the eastern megalopolis—New Jersey and the two great cities that bracket it—alone or with a friend. Some of the landscapes I traveled have already changed; I describe them as I experienced them. Reflecting a New Jerseyan's geographical imagination, the book is constructed with the stories of New Jersey (Part II) surrounded by those of New York City (Part I) and Philadelphia (Part III).

This book takes place on my turf, on my terrain. I hope it demonstrates that when we adventure through our own neighborhood we do so profoundly. I'm not sure what *human ecology* means, but I like the term and mean to appropriate it. Maybe it's a way of embracing one's own land. This book is a love letter to my much abused land.

PART ONE

NEW YORK CITY

Big City Waters

Ah, what can ever be more stately and admirable
to me than mast-hemmed Manhattan?
River and sunset and scallop-edged waves of
flood tide?

WALT WHITMAN, "CROSSING BROOKLYN FERRY"

If one is intent on urban adventure, a natural place to begin might be New York City, the Big Apple, the mother of all urban adventure sites. New York's geography is endlessly fascinating. Four-fifths of the city is on islands surrounded by the ocean and great rivers; some thirty bridges angle across the waterways between the boroughs. As solid as it seems, New York is a liquid place, bearing more than a passing resemblance to Venice.

At the center of things, surrounded by water, the capital of the world but still an island, is Manhattan. Oblivious to its massive stone skyscrapers, waters rush by Manhattan's supine body on all sides—the Hudson on its western flank, the East and Harlem rivers along its eastern, with Spuyten Duyvil Creek rounding its head and New York Harbor, the beginnings of the Atlantic Ocean, resplendent at its feet. Like any island, Manhattan almost asks to be circumnavigated. I wondered: Could one circle Manhattan by canoe? More than once I had taken the tourist boat trip around the island, but now I fancied making the trip on my own.

Well, not entirely on my own. A canoe is a tricky enough proposition without attempting a solo expedition anywhere, much less when you're a rank amateur not entirely sure which end of the canoe is which and when you plan to travel through big city waters. If you sit at either end of a canoe, the other end lifts and catches every breeze like a sail; you're in constant danger of tipping over. And if you step into a canoe on one end, you're likely to fly right out of it into the water. This happened to me one summer on a Maine pond to the eternal delight of my watching children. The only safe way to pilot a canoe solo is by kneeling amidships, Indian-style, J-stroking all the while to keep yourself going straight, but that position and activity would precipitate knee surgery long before you made it around Manhattan.

Who then would go with me? My wife, Patricia, companion of choice in virtually all of life's other adventures, is an unrepentant antagonist of the great outdoors. She is a self-made woman—a lawyer by trade—and strong and tough-minded when she has to be, but she is the sworn enemy of all insects and variations of temperature greater than ten degrees. She encourages my adventures; she thought canoeing around Manhattan was "a fantastic idea." But it was the last thing in the world she wanted to do.

I asked Ralph Thompson, my next-door neighbor, if he was interested, and he fairly shouted, "Not a chance!" I was surprised by the vehemence of his reaction. I didn't know Ralph well, but he seemed a nice enough guy; our kids played together across the backyard fence.

Ralph said, "A canoe'll dissolve in those acid waters just like that. Phyttttt! One minute there's you and the canoe. The next, just some green and purple bubbles. And if the toxic water doesn't get you, you'll get hit by a ship. Man, there's ocean liners in New York Harbor!"

Ralph, I recalled then, is an insurance agent with State Farm. When I first knew him, I would kid him by singing the State Farm commercial—"Like a good neighbor / State Farm is there"— but Ralph would say "That's right" and never crack a smile.

I next called Phil Herbert. Phil is a big admirer of tales of heroic adventure. His favorite book is James Dickey's *Deliverance.* "Look," he said, "canoeing around Manhattan could be a lot worse than *Deliverance.*"

"What are you talking about?" I said to Phil. "The Statue of Liberty will take good care of us."

"The Statue of Liberty?" Phil laughed. "She's standing up there like an advertisement for Right Guard. Those guys in *Deliverance* got buggered, and they were just out in the woods. The Statue of Liberty won't do a thing when the muggers and buggers get us."

But I could tell that Phil was intrigued. And I was keen on Phil, because he's the kind of guy who will try anything. He's a survivalist without the right-wing politics; it's almost a religion with him. I also knew he had a yellow aluminum canoe stashed away under mountains of debris in his garage. Phil is the total out-of-doors freak. He has more outdoor gear than Hermann's sporting goods stores. "You got permission from anyone?" Phil asked.

This was a problem I had not anticipated. What if canoeing around Manhattan was against the law? Bikes aren't allowed on superhighways like the New Jersey Turnpike, so maybe canoes aren't allowed in the powerful waters around Manhattan. I began phoning various city agencies in the hope that, with permission granted, Phil would come with me.

But who you gonna call? The Parks Department suggested the Coast Guard. The Coast Guard suggested the police. The police referred me to the Port Authority. The Port Authority referred me back to the Coast Guard. This time the Coast Guard referred me to the offices of the several borough presidents through whose waters we would pass. I called the offices of the borough presidents of Manhattan, Brooklyn, Queens, and the Bronx. The first three referred me back to the Parks Department or the police, but a woman in the Bronx borough president's office said, "You need a permit."

"How do I get it?" I asked.

"You have to fill out a form."

"Can you send me the form, please?"

"The man who handles forms is on vacation," she said, stifling a yawn.

It was hopeless. If I persisted, I might eventually get a definitive answer from some city agency, and it would probably be no. The surer course was just to do it. If you want to do anything out of the ordinary in this world, don't ask permission, because there's always someone who will say no.

Let's face it, there are two kinds of people in this world: can-do people and can't-do people. Can't-do people usually work in government or for insurance companies, like my neighbor Ralph. Insurance people are the ultimate can't-do people because they don't want you doing anything, leastwise anything interesting or exciting. Not that they're truly interested in your health and safety; they just want to go on collecting premiums from you forever and never have to pay off. The one person I'm absolutely certain is glad I'm alive is a guy who sold me a life insurance policy twenty-five years ago. I've moved six times since then, but his annual birthday cards never fail to reach me. They're just like other birthday cards, but there's a covert message: "Glad you're alive; keep sending the premiums."

Insurance people will insure you against anything—poverty, bad marriages, meteors hitting your house. For a high enough premium I'll bet you can even get them to guarantee your immortality. An Argentine I wrote my first book on, D. F. Sarmiento, said in 1847 that the great thing about the United States was, if you wanted to do something dangerous, even kill yourself, nobody would stop you. Not anymore.

I phoned Phil Herbert and began to tell him of my travails gaining permission for the trip. Phil interrupted and said, "Why are you so uptight about a permit?"

"What?" I said.

"Let's just go. I've already got the canoe out of the garage."

"Right," I said, deciding on the instant not to mention who it was that sent me off on my adventures within the New York City bureaucracy.

One thing you should know about Phil and me: we're opposites—which is maybe why we get along so well. He's Irish-Catholic and I'm Jewish, and we have a kind of Abie's Irish Rose relationship. If Phil were a woman and I wasn't married to Patricia, I would marry him. I envy Phil his easy anticlericalism. He went through eight grades of parochial school, so he knows life is absurd and doesn't worry about it. Five thousand years of history and the Six Million keep me worrying about it.

Phil makes me laugh, which is the nicest thing I can say about anyone. We probably exaggerate our differences for the fun of it. Phil plays the hard-bitten misanthrope with me, and I the bright-eyed, bushy-tailed optimist with him. I told Phil this trip would make us the modern-day Lewis and Clark. "More like Mutt and Jeff," he responded.

Phil is a fireman, but he reads more books than anyone I know. His character incorporates both sides of the Irish stereo-type: half responsible, serious FBI man with shiny black shoes; half falling-down-drunk poet.

I've always liked Phil's spur-of-the-moment approach to life. Me, I make lists. Sometimes, when consolidation would be too daunting a task, I even make a list list, a kind of concordance to my lists. It'll say something like: #1 list under magnet on refrig-erator, #2 list on dresser, #3 list taped to bathroom mirror. Occa-sionally I can hear Patricia laughing somewhere in the house, and I know she's spotted one of my lists. She said to me once, "As long as your lists don't start to mate." I've even done some-thing—and here I confess to the reader what I have never told another human being—that wasn't on a list and, afterward, when no one was watching, got credit for it by putting the item on the list and immediately crossing it off.

Phil and I met years ago at a reading I was giving from one of my works at the Old York bookstore in New Brunswick. His comments after my performance were so sharp and, frankly, so flattering I invited him for a beer and we became friends. It was a long time before he told me he was a fireman. It was as if he was ashamed of being a fireman around intellectuals. Of course, when I learned he was a fireman, I was glad. I had been afraid he was, like me, another professor.

The inside of Phil's house is even more full of books than his garage is full of sports gear. It looks like he's perpetually getting ready to have a garage sale. Books are stacked up everywhere—not just on shelves but spilling out of the closets and onto the floor. There are even bookcases in the kitchen.

The most extreme example of Phil's book obsession is his bedside table. There the books are stacked a yard high, no exaggeration. More than one girlfriend has threatened to leave him because of those books on the bedside table. I sympathize with them. Imagine lovemaking under such precarious conditions! I keep telling Phil that he and some lovely are going to die one night when an avalanche from the bedside table rolls down onto the bed. "What a way to go," he says.

Phil doesn't just buy these books and stand them around to impress people; he reads them. Reading is one reason he's a fireman. More than any other occupation it gives him time to read. Down at the firehouse they call Phil "Shakespeare." I'll phone him there and hear someone yell, "Hey, Shakespeare, it's for you." They give Phil a hard time because he's always carrying a book around and reading between fires instead of playing cards with the boys.

I also get a hard time at work. The professors at the university where I teach think I'm not sufficiently scholarly. In the academy, if your courses are popular you must be pandering to the ignorant student masses and couldn't be scholarly. My colleagues consider writing scholarly only when it's unintelligible to normal humans and appears in unread, obscure journals. The top third of each page is text, the bottom two-thirds footnotes. Even proud mothers of such scholars, when sent their publications, try to read them and give up.

If Henry David Thoreau appeared today and applied for a position at my university, *Walden* prominently listed in his curriculum vitae, he'd be turned down—seen as a ne'er-do-well camper and hiker, not sufficiently scholarly.

Maybe I should have been a forest ranger or a fireman, like Phil. No doubt Phil and I represent to each other what each of us partly wishes he was. I admire Phil's common sense and dogged bravery, and I guess he admires my ideas. Phil wishes he was an intellectual—which, of course, he *is*—and I'm his link to the academy. As for me, well, Phil is my ambassador to the "rednecks."

Our canoe trip began on a warm Saturday afternoon in August at the Battery, where we parked Phil's old Ford station wagon with the canoe lashed to the top and went to have a look at the water. We had decided to begin on the Hudson, which is so wide we'd have no trouble steering around any obstacle. There was no point tackling the narrower confines of the Harlem and East rivers right at the start. At Phil's insistence, we had planned the trip to catch the tides. "Tides schmides," I had said, but Phil grimaced and pointed to his charts. As I would learn, it is impossible to make it up the Hudson in a canoe against the tides, which twice a day roll powerfully up the river 120 miles to Albany and then charge back down. "Try it," Phil said. "You'll end up in Africa."

We put the canoe in the water next to the fireboat house. Phil, being the stronger of us, got into the bow of the canoe. He pulled; I pushed and steered. The tide was coming in so strong you could see it and hear it smack against the wooden pilings. It barreled upriver and we went with it, moving up the Hudson with no more effort than it took to steer. You really believe in the moon's powers when you're in a tide. The Hudson was flowing upriver instead of down; that's all there was to it.

The water was also as choppy as the ocean, and wakes from passing garbage scows and tankers made it more so. But as long as we kept the prow of the canoe pointing into the waves, we did fine. It was scary though. Sometimes we went down so deep into a trough between swells we saw nothing but water; then, as we rose on the next wave, tall buildings popped up before us like great stone corks.

We passed the Circle Line pier, where a tourist boat was putting out from the wharf. Just upriver, the colossal proportions of the berthed aircraft carrier *Intrepid* loomed up out of the water. A sailor on the deck waved to us. At least I think he waved. He was so far above us, so tiny, it was hard to tell.

We kept rolling upriver. To our left were the high purple cliffs of the Jersey Palisades. To our right, block after block of Manhattan retreated behind us. Each time a bit of light flashed among the dense thickets of buildings on Riverside Drive, that was a block.

A police boat steamed past us downriver, and I hunkered down and tried to look inconspicuous. Phil shouted something to me over the wind, but his words rocketed before him upriver.

"Whadja say?" I asked.

Phil turned in his seat and repeated, "Maybe it's legal after all."

"Nah," I said. "They just don't know if it is or it isn't."

A minute later, the sound of diesels alerted us that the police boat was coming back. Uh oh.

It stopped two hundred feet away, and an amplified voice that nearly catapulted me out of the canoe said, "Put your life jacket on."

"We *have* . . . ," Phil started to yell, but then he turned and stared at me. My life jacket sat at my feet, in the bottom of the canoe. Sheepishly, under the full gaze of Phil and the police, I slipped the jacket on, and the police boat rumbled off downriver.

We passed Grant's grimy gray tomb high on the bluff. A strange place to stash a president; didn't Grant rate Washington, D.C.? Ten blocks farther north we spotted something white floating toward us on the surface of the water. As we got closer, I saw that it wasn't one object but a flotilla of hundreds of objects. "What's that?" Phil shouted.

"Looks like a school of jellyfish," I said. "Don't touch them. They sting."

As we came alongside the floating mass, Phil picked up one of the objects on his paddle. "Trojan, ribbed," he said. And now we were surrounded by a sea of condoms, each bobbing in the water and winking at us in the afternoon light. Had there been a safe-sex orgy in a community upriver? Was this a subliminal commercial for that then current movie, *Sea of Love*? I knew condoms were making a comeback in America, but this was ridiculous.

"You and your urban adventure," Phil shouted.

"What's it mean?" I said to Phil.

"What?"

"The condoms. What's it mean?" All those condoms had to

mean something, had to have some deep mythic significance. Some connection to Moby Dick?

"Why's it have to mean anything?" Phil said. "It's just a bunch of condoms. I thought you came on this trip to get *away* from the university."

The condoms floated away, and we continued upriver toward the towers of the George Washington Bridge, which, like everything else about the Hudson, is on a gigantic scale. Beneath the bridge, we examined the undersides of cars and trucks passing above us, a view you ordinarily don't have of them. The vehicles looked vulnerable, as if their private parts were exposed. It was like looking up the dresses of women on a staircase high above. I felt almost as if I should avert my eyes.

Soon after, the sun low over the Palisades, we reached the farthest limits of Manhattan. Making a right turn under the New York Central railroad bridge, which spans Manhattan and the Bronx just above the surface of the water, we passed into Spuyten Duyvil Creek.

Spuyten Duyvil brings Hudson River waters around the top of Manhattan, where they become the Harlem—not a separate river at all, but the branch of the Hudson that flows around the east side of the island. Some say the name Spuyten Duyvil is a corruption of the Dutch for Devil's Spout, but another interpretation is Spiting the Devil. In his *History of New York,* Washington Irving told of Anthony Van Corlear, who endeavored to swim across the fast-flowing waters to spite the devil but drowned in the attempt. A huge blue *C*, painted on the side of the gorge at a place called Split Rock, is near the spot where a Columbia University rowing team member also drowned in Spuyten Duyvil in 1976.

Spuyten Duyvil once flowed some blocks to the north, but in 1895 a new, enlarged ship canal was blasted through to replace it, the former Spuyten Duyvil was filled in, and Manhattan became shorter by two hundred yards. The Marble Hill neighborhood, named for its quarries, was now physically part of the Bronx—though it remained politically part of Manhattan, and its phone numbers appeared in the Manhattan directory, until only a few years ago.

Though Manhattan lost land in this instance, it has generally increased in size over time. Much of Lower Manhattan is filled-in land, including the recently created Battery Park City and World Financial Center, which were built on the fill from the nearby World Trade Center excavation. The propensity of the original Dutch settlers to push back the sea still seems to be carried in the genes of New Yorkers.

Luckily for us it was now slack tide in Spuyten Duyvil, as we needed quiet water to get out of the gorge. Luckily, too, there was a swampy spot on the Manhattan bank. We got out of the water there and, with our remaining strength, hauled the canoe up the cliff. Our plan was to camp overnight rather than chance descending the Harlem and East rivers in the dark. We could catch the next outgoing tide in the morning.

We put up the pup tent, wondering when someone had last pitched a tent in Manhattan. Quite possibly it was erected right where we were—Inwood Hill Park, the site of the last Native American settlement on the island and where arrowheads are still found. Phil wondered what the Indians would have thought of the New York City park sign that greeted us with its huge "No" followed by a long list of prohibited activities. Luckily, there was nothing on the list about stashing canoes in the bushes; the Parks Department hadn't reckoned on invasions from the sea. "Entering Park after Dusk" was, however, high on the list: number 3.

We had food with us but decided a fire would make us too easily detectable. Besides, we were both in the mood for a good meal and a little nightlife. As darkness closed in, we took a flashlight and, on unsteady land legs, made our way out of the park and onto Broadway, where Clancy's Bar & Grill stared us in the face.

Phil and I got a bottle of wine and some steaks. All the time we were in Clancy's I kept fancying myself a participant in that old TV show *I've Got a Secret*. I kept staring at the waitress's pantie line under her tight white uniform and wishing she would ask me something, anything at all. I wanted to tell her that Phil and I had just emerged from the waters of Spuyten Duyvil. But she never asked us anything about who we were or where we came from. I mean we could have been enemy spies or something. We could have been terrorists loaded with plastic explosives, put ashore by a submarine. Finally, I couldn't stand it anymore. "You may not believe this," I said as she finished reciting the list of desserts, "but we're camping out in the park across the street."

"That's nice," she said.

"*Nice?*" I said to Phil when she had moved off to get our pies. "Couldn't she do better than *nice?*"

"Whadja want her to do, cheer?"

"Well, maybe a little appreciation."

"Forget it," Phil said. "On a river trip there's no point talking to anyone on the banks. Every time Huck and Jim talked to anyone on the banks they got into trouble."

But I was miffed the waitress hadn't admired our exploits. Shameful as it is to admit, there must still have been a part of me that equated canoeing around Manhattan with, say, leaping to catch the winning pass in the end zone, no time left on the clock, and all the women pouring out of the stands and jumping on me. The incident with the waitress suggested that women didn't care one hoot whether I caught passes or canoed around Manhattan. I knew Patricia didn't. But we men go on playing our little games.

After dinner, we took a cab downtown and saw a movie. It hardly mattered to us *which* movie. It was fun just to have snuck onto the land to see any kind of movie in the middle of a canoe trip.

"Where you going with that flashlight?" the blue-haired lady in the ticket booth wanted to know. Maybe she thought we intended to usurp the usher's job or disturb the other patrons by shining the flashlight around the darkened theater. "Oh, that?" I said. "Been shopping. Not to worry."

We really needed the flashlight when we returned uptown and walked into the park. It was so dark we couldn't find our tent and canoe. "Bastards stole them," Phil said. Someone must have seen us arrive and, the moment we quit the park, made off with our gear.

But we had been looking in the wrong place. Stumbling around in the dark almost an hour, we finally slid down a rock outcropping and tripped over our tent, which was pitched in the clearing at its base. What was it doing there, our canoe too? Things seemed so different in the night; I could have sworn our stuff had been moved.

Phil had some cigars, and we sat on a rock ledge overlooking Spuyten Duyvil and peacefully smoked them and looked at the water and the rising moon. Here we were in Manhattan, the most intense spot on the globe, but you couldn't know a more profound solitude. Night creatures moved in the bushes. An opossum—an animal I was familiar with only as a flattened highway object—ran into the clearing, looked at us, and darted out of sight again. Life seemed real good.

In the morning we had Pop Tarts and orange juice in cardboard containers and spooned up a whole jar of Smucker's Gooberjelly using plastic spoons. Gooberjelly is great stuff to take on a trip because you have the peanut butter and jelly together in the same jar and don't need anything else, not even bread. But how I wished we'd saved some juice, because I had a gob of Gooberjelly stuck halfway down and nothing to wash it along unless I cared to suck up some of the PCBs floating on Spuyten Duyvil. My lungs felt like they were cemented together with Crazy Glue.

"Want me to do a Heimlich on you?" Phil asked.

"No," I croaked.

"How about a whack? Should I whack you a good one on the back?"

Before I could answer, Phil hit me hard on the back with the flat of his hand, and the Gooberjelly headed south.

"Where'd you learn to do that?" I asked Phil gratefully.

"Hey, man, I'm a fireman," he replied. "You call 911, you get 911."

We lowered the canoe into Spuyten Duyvil and continued on

our way. Rounding the corner of Manhattan, we passed under the Broadway bridge, where a train was rattling overhead into the Bronx, and started down the Harlem River.

A short way down the Harlem the massive structure of George Washington High School rose up over my shoulder on the rocky promontory, inspiring one of my scale-the-nearest-cliff fantasies. I yelled to Phil about it, but he just turned and gave me a look. Across the river, on the Bronx bank, the massive Kingsbridge Veterans Hospital appeared and, soon after, Yankee Stadium.

Unlike the Hudson, the city crowds in from both banks on the Harlem and East rivers. Helicopters roar overhead down the rivers, and the water traffic is brisk. Tugboats and small tankers are thick in there, and we worked hard to stay out of their way. A guide on a Circle Line tourist boat must have said something about us over the loudspeakers, because the passengers cheered and waved wildly to us as we swept by.

But there was no time to bask in glory. The Harlem was about to join the East River at a place ominously called Hell Gate. We had been warned about this spot. There are whirlpools and vicious currents, and shipwrecks have taken place at Hell Gate. The East River, not a river at all but a tidal strait, drains Long Island Sound, and the confluence of its waters and those of the Harlem in such a narrow space creates great turbulence. It's as if the energy of Hell Gate exemplifies the spirit of New York—the collision of endless immigrants with the city's shores, the vast multitudes streaming through the streets.

We decided to hug the Manhattan bank, as far away from the swirling waters as we could get. With the added protection of Mill Rock, a tiny island that juts from the river offshore, we got through all right—though several times the canoe was tugged this way or that by an unseen hand.

Just ahead on the grassy bank was Gracie Mansion, the mayor's residence, a vestige of eighteenth-century New York. Distracted by this genteel sight, we inattentively entered the channel alongside Roosevelt Island. No one had mentioned the dangers of this channel, but it was here that all the turbulence we feared at Hell Gate became a reality. So narrowed was the river by the island that the water rushed through as if coming out of a hose. We rode the watery roller coaster, struggling desperately not to keel over or smack into the concrete bulwark. If anything got in our way here, a boat, a floating log, we were finished. For almost two miles we hung on, moving perilously fast, with the tides and current rushing us madly toward the sea.

Then, as we passed under the cable car and Roosevelt Island ended, the East River assumed its customary width and demeanor, and we breathed normally. We were able to enjoy the United Nations, which has a grace from the water one doesn't experience on First Avenue. Passersby on the walkways above Franklin Delano Roosevelt Drive yelled things at us, but the wind carried their words over our heads.

We passed under the baroque iron framework of the Manhattan Bridge, then under the gothic towers and finespun cables of the venerable Brooklyn Bridge. We could smell the Fulton Fish Market just ahead, so we knew the southern tip of Manhattan was fast approaching. We had to slow down. Otherwise, we would shoot past the end of the island and be dragged out to sea.

We decided to play it safe. Hugging the land, we painstakingly crawled from pier to pier, careful not to let the waves smack us against the barnacle-encrusted piles. In this manner, we crept around the wide foot of Manhattan and, after so many watery miles, were back at the Battery.

But the tides were rushing out as fast in the Hudson as in the East River, and now they were against us. Although we paddled our hardest to make it upriver the short distance to Phil's station wagon, we couldn't move. It took all our energy just to stay in place. Phil tried using the bow rope to lasso the huge bolts on the piles. Once he actually caught one of them and pulled us forward fifteen feet, but Phil was no cowboy and, after what seemed like fifty more tries, gave up. "Damn," I said. But I had no idea how to move the canoe upriver either.

We briefly considered tying on to a pier and waiting some hours for the tide to change, but the sun was frying us and, besides, we both needed a bathroom pronto. "Let's just say we did it," Phil said. "I won't tell if you don't." So we never did quite circumnavigate Manhattan; thirty-one miles and we couldn't make the last hundred yards because of the tides.

While Phil found this amusing, I felt like a failure. "You are one goal-oriented son of a bitch," Phil said. "Lighten up. Someday you'll think the most interesting thing about this trip is that we didn't quite make it."

This has proven to be true. Failures, disasters even, make the best stories, and I know that whenever I tell anyone about the trip around Manhattan I never fail to mention, with great good humor, missing our goal by only one hundred yards. But back then, as I climbed the fifteen-foot rock seawall behind Phil, with my share of our gear in one arm and the bow rope tied to my belt, I was depressed.

We were up now, but how to get our vessel up the wall? Even without the tides tugging at the canoe, it was a straight up, eighty-pound lift. While we cogitated on this problem, I held tight to the bow rope; if I let go for a second, that canoe was history.

After several fancy and failed attempts, employing what we remembered from high school physics (much discussion about fulcrums and pulleys and block and tackle), we simply grasped the bow rope and pulled the canoe straight up the wall on its keel, oblivious to the indignant shrieks of the aluminum. Phil's canoe bears the scars to this day.

Getting the canoe up had been such a challenge that I forgot my disappointment over missing our goal and cheered up. We loaded our gear into the canoe and portaged it across Battery Park.

A homeless guy sat sunbathing on a park bench, his belongings neatly stashed in an A & P shopping basket. He stared at us, wide-eyed. "Say," he said.

"Yeah?" Phil replied.

"Where'd you all come from?"

I was delighted. I had struck out with the waitress the night before, but here, at last, was someone interested in our trip.

But before I could begin what might have been a lengthy

discourse on New York City geography—on tides and currents and the beauty of the city as seen from the water—Phil, as if asserting again his idea that we should avoid contact with people on the banks, short-circuited me. "Europe," he said. Then we lashed the canoe atop Phil's station wagon with rubber bungee cords and headed for the Holland Tunnel and home.

2

Copping a Pee in the Big Apple

Every walk is a sort of crusade.

HENRY DAVID THOREAU, "WALKING"

After a long, dull winter, I was, as spring approached, eager for another adventure. Having canoed around Manhattan with Phil Herbert, I decided this time to experience the island on foot and by myself. Walking is something you almost have to do by yourself—unless you're sauntering or strolling, which isn't what I had in mind. I wanted to *hike* Manhattan. I saw the island as a physical challenge.

An invitation to lunch at Windows on the World, high up in the World Trade Center, provided the inspiration for the trip. I was not a very good guest. During the meal I repeatedly got up from the table and circled the room, staring through the thick glass at the sparkling scenes below: the traffic creeping along the vast avenues, the waterways at the fish-shaped island's edges—the same powerful waterways along which Phil and I had struggled the previous summer, now, from such a height, silver and still.

Seeing Manhattan whole and at once was breathtaking. Prior to my water adventure, I had known only the dark canyons between skyscrapers; I had spent considerable time on certain floors in certain buildings. I took cabs; I took subways. Occasionally, when the weather was good, I walked some blocks, but always toward some specific destination.

In Manhattan one rushes about as if pursued. Anyone who bucks the frantic pace even for a moment—to examine an architectural detail or to observe the street life—is assumed to be up to no good. I had never just gone for a walk in Manhattan. It had never occurred to me, say, that one might stroll across the narrow island from river to river for the pleasure of it.

Manhattan is not like Paris or London or Budapest, where the fluvial scene is the center of city life and where the best restaurants and great palaces look out on the river. Close by most of Manhattan's waters people are rarely seen on the streets. Crime is high, real estate values low. Manhattan is strangely inverted, its wealth concentrated in its interior avenues. Despite its vitality, Manhattan is more mausoleum than island. It turns away from the very source of its aliveness—its finest feature, its waterways.

Now, staring down in amazement at all I beheld, it was Manhattan as a real island that most impressed itself upon me. A fourteen-mile expanse of land breathed, surrounded by powerful waterways. Beneath the steel and concrete encrustations were geological and biological forces that might erupt anytime humans relaxed their guard. The island had its own topography, its own flora and fauna, and, because of the heat it gives off and the wind currents inspired by its tall buildings, its own weather. I wanted to know that island, to embrace it, to claim it for my own. I decided that, as soon as I had the opportunity, I would hike Manhattan from one end to the other, to view the island this time not from its rivers but from its sidewalks.

A month later, when I had a free Saturday, I awoke at dawn and, leaving Patricia and the children sleeping, took the bus into the city and then the Broadway IRT train to the northern tip of the island. It seemed the right end of Manhattan from which to start. From the 268-foot eminence of Fort Tryon Park, the island slopes gradually to the south, paralleling the course of the rivers that run at its flanks. If ever so imperceptibly, descending only inches per block, I would have the advantage of traveling down instead of uphill.

With hiking boots on my feet and a knapsack on my back, I got on Broadway, originally an American Indian trail, later called Breede Wegh by the Dutch. It is Manhattan's spine, the only street that runs the entire length of the island, Spuyten Duyvil to the Battery. The other avenues are of later vintage and straight, but Broadway meanders down the island, breaking Manhattan's gridlike uniformity here and there, creating wedge-shaped open places such as Times Square where it crosses other avenues and sometimes even dictating the shape of structures such as the Flatiron Building.

Broadway is 275 blocks long, a daunting distance. But unlike a wilderness trail, where you're never sure you've reached the right boulder or blazed tree, street signs on Broadway tell you exactly where you are and how far you have to go. The blocks clip along, and you get into a rhythm: step off the curb, mount the other curb, glide on down the sidewalk to the next corner, and do it all over again. Your spirits are kept up because you know you're making progress.

Raw and blustery weather also kept me moving that March day—to stay warm if nothing else. Crazed wind currents charged between the buildings, carrying newspapers through the air and along the sidewalks. They stuck to fences and wrapped themselves around my calves like city tumbleweed. I stopped to peel them off, not always successfully resisting the desire to read. When you're out-of-doors and doing something vigorous, a piece of print has an appeal it can never have in a library.

Moving down Upper Broadway, I was struck by the fact that the neighborhoods seemed eminently middle-class, contradicting the tourist books, which suggest that only the very rich and very poor live in Manhattan. Another common misconception is that Manhattan above 100th Street is exclusively black and Puerto Rican, but this is because visitors confine themselves to Midtown and points south, rarely venturing to the northern reaches of the island. Here I was passing Mulligan's Grocery and then an old friend from the canoe trip with Phil, Clancy's Bar & Grill. By the time I got into the 190s, I'd passed two synagogues and a Jewish hospital. It wasn't until the 180s that I heard Spanish spoken, and I was well into the 160s before I saw many blacks. Descending Manhattan, you pass through ethnic groups like an archaeologist slicing through strata of civilizations.

You also go over many hills, a reminder that the word Manhattan is derived from the Algonquin word meaning island of the hills. Automobile shock absorbers take a terrific beating in Manhattan because drivers just bounce along, oblivious to the island's steep rises and falls. No wonder those big yellow taxicabs only last a year.

Originally the island was a series of mountains, but these were eroded during the ice ages by glaciers that covered Manhattan to the height of today's skyscrapers. Erosion continues, but now it's the buildings, streets, and sidewalks that erode instead of the paved-over hills—almost as if developers have sheathed the island in asphalt and stone to protect it from the elements.

I was especially aware of Manhattan's hilliness as I descended Broadway from Washington Heights into what geologists call the Manhattanville Valley. The bottom of the valley, at 125th Street, lies, like most major Manhattan cross streets, in a dip or fault in the rock. The dip is so extreme here that the Broadway subway emerges from Washington Heights and continues as an elevated train for only a few blocks before reentering the ground on the opposite hillside, Morningside Heights.

At 125th Street I encountered some "wildlife." Quite improbably, a rooster was running along Broadway, fleeing from cars but afraid to mount the sidewalk, where children taunted it. Across Broadway, a merchant sweeping the sidewalk stopped to watch; above him a woman with fat arms leaned out of her third-floor window. Had the rooster fluttered out of a truck bound for market? Was it a fighting cock, escaped from some nearby barrio pit?

Suddenly, a taxi hit the rooster, and the shower of feathers was accompanied by a universal sigh of remorse. The taxi driver got out of the cab, inspected the rooster, and drove off. A small brown boy stepped off the curb and delicately lifted the rooster's limp head, hoping to discover some sign of life. "*Dios mío,*" he cried. Then he and his comrades, heads down, moved sadly off down the street.

Originally Manhattan was full of real wildlife. A certain Jan Jansen shot the bears that prowled his orchards in the vicinity of where Pine Street is today, and Beaver Street, also in Lower

Manhattan, is named for the many beavers that built dams in the streams and marshes that once predominated in its vicinity.

Nowadays it's fashionable to say that the only wildlife on Manhattan island are the muggers, but actually there are still some nonhuman wild animals—quite apart from obvious examples like the water rats in Central Park's ponds and the strange breed of cats that inhabit the tunnels under Grand Central Terminal. Owls and pheasants occasionally are spotted in Inwood Hill Park, where Phil and I camped on our around-Manhattan canoe trip, and muskrats often are seen swimming along the banks of Spuyten Duyvil. Vixens and their young have been seen cavorting just yards off the Henry Hudson Parkway.

Manhattan also has a large population of starlings, nesting high in the cornices of the skyscrapers, which emerge at evening to keep the island's insect population down. Hawks headquarter there too and, like Batman, swoop down the stone and glass canyons from time to time to pick off a pigeon. It's as if only predatory animals can flourish on Manhattan.

This would apply to Manhattan's "alligators." According to the story, vacationers brought baby alligators back from Florida as pets. But when they grew too big for aquariums—and too pesky in family bathtubs—they were dropped into the sewers, where they thrived. This legend inspired the 1980 film *Alligator,* in which just such a Floridian import grows to monumental size in the sewers, emerging from time to time to devour a citizen and terrorize the city. Some New Yorkers still believe alligators are under the city, eyes gleaming in the darkness, waiting for a hapless Con Edison worker.

In addition to its wildlife, Manhattan has some remarkable plant life—and not just in the parks. The ginkgo, oldest known tree species, flourishes in a gritty traffic island down the center of Upper Broadway. Virtually impervious to disease and pollution, the ginkgo has survived since the age of the dinosaurs. Like Manhattan's wildlife, it's tough enough to withstand the ravages of civilization.

The ailanthus, New York's chief weed tree, also thrives on the Broadway island, as well as in vacant lots all over the city. It is the streetwise tree celebrated in Betty Smith's 1943 novel *A Tree Grows in Brooklyn.* The ailanthus is tough and grows fast. I know one that sprouted from a tar joint and, aided by the drip from an air conditioner two stories above, began to push a small building off its foundation before anyone knew it was there.

Scaling Morningside Heights, I passed Columbia University and Barnard College. The farther south I went, the more animated the streets became. Pawnshops and ethnic restaurants sprouted colorful awnings, record shops blared reggae and rap. Despite being concerned about the passing time, I wasn't able to entirely resist window-shopping. In fact, I saw a neat leather safari hat in a shop and went in and would have bought it if I'd had enough money with me.

There were crowds of people now on the sidewalk for me to get around, sometimes strolling four or five abreast. What was the matter with these people? Didn't they know I was no ordinary pedestrian but an urban adventurer on an expedition with many miles of blocks to go?

And then there were the red lights. Farther north they hadn't mattered much, but here, what with all the people and traffic, red lights seriously interfered with my rhythm. Sometimes I would be making a block a minute and then have to stand two minutes waiting for a light to change.

I learned that the best time to cross the street is not when the light turns green. When it turns green, cars whip around the corner and get you. It's actually safer in New York to cross the street when you have a red light and nothing's coming; and the very best time to cross the street is just as the light turns red, before cars in the cross streets gun their motors and whip across the intersection.

I once lived in Minneapolis and was shocked when I jaywalked and the cars heading in both directions came to a halt. It was as if I had been transformed into a school bus with red lights flashing and stop sign extended. I soon learned to cross Minneapolis streets according to the rules. But you wouldn't want to cross New York City streets according to the rules. In New York, following the rules will get you killed.

At 93rd Street, where a blind street musician was performing on a saxophone, I crossed over to the Broadway island and sat on a bench to rest. The back of my left foot, just above the heel, hurt terribly—the result, I imagined, of all that going up and down curbs, mile after mile, a hazard peculiar to urban hiking. I took off my boot and massaged my foot.

Then I got my lunch out of my knapsack and greedily devoured it: an apple, a candy bar, and a peanut butter and jelly sandwich—not Gooberjelly this time, just a plain old peanut butter and jelly sandwich. Will I ever be too old for peanut butter and jelly? I wondered. In terms of pure pleasure provided human beings, the peanut butter and jelly sandwich has got to be one of the great inventions of history. What did children (and some adults) eat before peanut butter and jelly?

Two blocks from where I was sitting, at 93rd Street and Riverside Drive, a huge chrysoberyl crystal weighing ten pounds was found during a construction project. It's now in the Museum of Natural History, where they have a collection of Manhattan semiprecious stones in dusty cases, including the largest garnet ever found in North America. There are also rare minerals in Manhattan. Under the West Side Highway lies a deposit of uranium so potent it has been known to activate a Geiger counter in a car passing far overhead.

If its real estate weren't so valuable, Manhattan would probably be mined. Much is known about Manhattan's geology because of all the excavation for subways, sewers, and buildings and all the tunnels that honeycomb the island. A popular fear is that Manhattan will sink someday under the weight of all its skyscrapers, but the rock and compacted earth removed for a foundation is always heavier than the building erected on a site. Buildings are like compartmentalized steel ships: mostly air. Manhattan is actually getting lighter all the time. It's more likely to float away than sink.

Finishing my lunch, I limped south and soon came to Columbus Circle, where the skyscrapers begin. The tall buildings of Manhattan appear to cover the island, but they're actually located only in two places: at Midtown, where the Empire State

Building is found, and in Lower Manhattan, where the World Trade Center stands. Skyscrapers have to be anchored to rock, and at these two places the bedrock is close to the surface. The World Trade Center would have cost twice as much in Greenwich Village because they'd have had to dig down so much farther. The toughest thing about erecting a skyscraper is digging the foundation in such close quarters and then having to dispose of all the material that's been excavated. I like the fact that, in Manhattan, you still have to be mindful of such basic things.

At that moment, however, I was glad that, in Manhattan, there are also less basic things present, such as telephones. I wanted to call home. That's something you can do on an urban hike you can't do in the wilderness. Calling home midway in my adventure seemed a grand thing to do. I would see how everyone was and then maybe slip in a brief, heroic comment about my foot, get a little sympathy—why not?

I wished I could have found a genuine phone booth, with a door I could close, but there were only these ratty little outdoor phones on the corner of 57th Street, utterly devoid of charm and offering no privacy—the equivalent in phone booths of McDonald's in food. You wouldn't even want to make an obscene call from such a phone.

The first phone I tried was broken. Well, more than broken: the receiver had been torn out, and only a dangling wire remained. The next phone seemed intact, but there was still that inescapable racket on Broadway to contend with. Taxis jockeyed for position and honked their horns nonstop. The wind was blowing a gale. "Where are you?" Patricia asked.

She said Joshua had awakened that morning with an ear infection; they had just returned from the pediatrician. This cast a bit of a pall on my expedition. I thought: What kind of father is out doing nothing more consequential than walking the length of Manhattan when his son has an ear infection? It would probably be my fault if he grew up deaf. I said something about this, and Patricia reminded me that I would have ample opportunity to atone for my "sins" the next day, when I was in charge of the kids. Besides, Joshua was already on the penicillin and was napping comfortably. That made me feel a bit better. Still, I decided not to say anything about my foot.

Moving southward, I entered the theater district. Some of the people in the streets—sidewalk peddlers, religious zealots, drug pushers, hookers—reminded me of my earlier reflections on Manhattan wildlife. As I passed a doorway, a well-dressed young man, looking like he could have been a Mormon missionary, asked quietly, "Anything?"

"What?" I said.

"Anything?"

"Whadya mean?"

"A girl?"

"No thanks."

"A boy?"

"No thanks," I said. "I'm just walking."

He followed me down the street. "Whereya walking?" he said.

"Just walking."

"Just walking?"

"Yeah."

"*Just?*"

"Yeah, just!" What was this guy, a shrink? Was there some shameful significance to my just walking? I could have told him I was hiking the island, involved him in my adventure as I had wanted to involve the waitress and homeless guy during the around-Manhattan canoe trip. But this enterprising fellow no doubt would then have said, "I told you you weren't just walking," and would have continued to pressure me.

He did anyway. "Some smoke?" he continued.

"No thanks."

"Smack?"

"No."

"Anything?" this persistent merchant repeated in a tone suggesting the implausibility of my not craving at least one of his wares.

Actually, I did have a need, but he couldn't fulfill it. For blocks I had been seeking a public restroom only to be reminded how user-unfriendly Manhattan is in this regard. If you don't live in Manhattan or work in Manhattan or if you aren't staying in a hotel in Manhattan, you can pretty well pee in your pants in Manhattan for all the city cares. Of course, if you appear respectable, it's a fairly simple matter to enter a hotel lobby or restaurant and pretend to be a patron; dressed as I was, forget it.

Desperate, I wandered down an alley between a delicatessen and a newsstand and wet down the dumpster they had parked back there, which, given its customary function, had a certain appropriateness for my crime. The relief was almost equaled by the pleasure that always attends getting away with something a trifle illegal—in this case, copping a pee in Manhattan. Nevertheless, the voice of conscience whispered: What would become of New York if everyone peed in alleys?

I have since learned how commonplace my experience was. My cousin tells me he was once reduced to peeing down an incinerator shaft in a Park Avenue apartment building when, by prearrangement, he arrived at a friend's apartment house with two cups of coffee in his bladder, got past the doorman, took the elevator to the twenty-sixth floor, and discovered his friend was not yet home. I wonder what a woman would have done in such a circumstance. A literary acquaintance is fond of saying that "New York is worse than Dickens's London when it comes to public accommodations." The mayor of New York had best pay attention. Maybe I'll send him a copy of the book with this passage circled in magic marker.

With one physical problem attended to, I looked to minimize the other, the agony in my left foot. Maybe I could focus on something outside myself—the Lamaze technique of urban hiking. The Empire State Building, which loomed ahead, seemed a worthy enough object. But the closer I got, the more difficult keeping it in view became. Lesser buildings blocked it the way mountains disappear once you get into their foothills.

This is a problem all over Manhattan. The most interesting parts of buildings, up high where the minarets and gargoyles and other decorative details are affixed, can't be seen except sometimes at a distance. Determined, nevertheless, to see the Empire

State close up, I stopped an elderly man alongside a gray building on 34th Street and asked him if he knew where it was.

This cantankerous gentleman regarded me with suspicion. "Dis a joke?" he demanded through the stub of a cigar that decorated his face.

I assured him it was not.

"You sure? I can take a joke."

"It's not a joke," I insisted. "I don't know where the Empire State Building is. I want to see it."

"It's right dere, dummy!" he shouted, pointing straight up in the air and moving quickly to put some distance between us.

Broadway passed through the garment district, Madison Square Park, and Union Square Park. The street numbers were getting low, but then I reached Greenwich Village and was reminded that there is still a large hunk of the island south of 1st Street. When the street numbers end, the old street names take over.

The cast-iron buildings of Soho offered a pleasant diversion. One of them sported a coffeehouse full of plants and paintings, and I went in thinking, hike or not, I was going to have a civilized cup of tea. I felt like a grizzled mountain man among the *culturati* and hoped no one could see that, under the long tablecloth, I had taken off my left boot and was stroking my foot.

Refreshed, I got back on the "Broadway Trail." At Canal Street I remembered that this was once a marsh where the Hudson and East River tides converged. A canal was dug in 1821 to drain the area, and it's still down there, flowing beneath the street.

Originally, Manhattan had some two dozen brooks and streams. Henry Hudson spoke of the beauty of the island's streams, which washed down from its heights into the rivers and harbor. Some of them still flow. You can hear them in the storm sewers if you know where to listen.

I passed City Hall Park, then Trinity Church, for some years the tallest building on the island. I was now at Wall Street, once the limit of European settlement, named for the stockade built along it for protection against Indian attacks. Contrary to popular belief, Native Americans went on living in the northern reaches of Manhattan for a century after Peter Minuit "bought" the island from them in 1626 for twenty-four dollars worth of beads and trinkets. Intermittent warfare between Europeans and Indians continued for much of that century.

I could now see open sky beyond the buildings, marking the end of the island. Good thing, too, because it was almost dark, and I felt more than a little vulnerable as I limped along. The streets were virtually deserted. I understood how elderly or infirm people must feel in the city streets, for I was manifestly aware of my potential as a target. It wasn't just the limp; I was stiff all over and could not have run from, much less fought off, a mugger. I felt like one of Manhattan's pigeons cowering under imminent attack from a hawk. But, whatever the risk, I wanted to reach the very tip of the island. No almosts, as in Phil's and my trip around Manhattan.

A tall, very dark black man crossed the street and advanced toward me. Was this it? Trying too hard to act cool and not betray my pain, I tripped and pitched headlong down the sidewalk. Pain shot through my right knee.

Now I'd done it! I heard the man running toward me and shielded my head with my hands. But instead of hitting me, the man asked, in what sounded like a Jamaican accent, "You all right? That was a nasty fall." He helped me to my feet. "You all right now?" I nodded my head in agreement, still in shock from my collision with the concrete. "You sure?" He dusted me off.

The right knee of my jeans was torn and the knee itself lacerated and bleeding. "I always keep a Band-Aid in my wallet," the man said, proceeding to peel the Band-Aid and, stooping, apply it to my knee. My knee hurt awfully, but not as much as recognizing that after years in the civil rights movement and contributing to every liberal cause and being able to claim that some of my best friends were indeed black and having once spent two days with Martin Luther King, I had, when the chips were down, revealed the racism that still lurked within me. *That* really hurt.

Chastened, the wind in my face, I finally reached the improbable address of One Broadway. Number One, *numero uno*! Of course, it was just a building; nobody was waiting there to hand me a trophy or even a bumper sticker. The last building on Broadway, the last building on the island, was closed and dark.

I crossed Manhattan's final street and entered Battery Park. No one else was in the park. Castle Clinton, the key feature of an offshore island long ago joined to Manhattan by fill, loomed up in front of me, and I knew that off to the right somewhere was the spot where Phil and I had pulled our canoe up the seawall.

Reaching the water's edge, I stood there with mixed feelings. I had been on an ambulatory roller coaster for 275 city blocks and was high from the experience, reluctant to climb back down.

But it was also glorious to have reached the end of the island. An ocean liner moved silently out to sea. The Statue of Liberty looked as if it envied the ship its mobility and would soon stride after it—even if that meant sinking massively beneath the waves. The lights were coming on in New Jersey. The view was unreal in its beauty, especially gratifying since I had walked so far to see it. It was like standing on the edge of the world.

Up the Creek to Manhattan

You will go with the water and . . . have
adventures.

HOLLING CLANCY HOLLING,
PADDLE-TO-THE-SEA

"Want to do it again?" I asked, when I phoned Phil Herbert the next summer.

"Sure, Don Quixote," he replied. Phil often calls me "Don Quixote," though he is, in his own way, as much of a dreamer as I am; neither of us would make a decent Sancho Panza. He continued: "Only this time we make it a bit more sporting, right? We canoe around Manhattan backward; we use our hands instead of paddles."

"Be quiet and listen," I said. "I don't want to canoe *around* Manhattan. I want to canoe *to* Manhattan."

"From Jersey? Like on what, the Turnpike?"

Phil was right: most of New Jersey is paved. And the New Jersey Turnpike is the state's automotive Mississippi. But the day before this conversation with Phil I had been studying a road map of New Jersey and Greater New York and noticed these thin blue lines wandering over its surface. At first, I thought they were back roads, "blue highways," but they were too wiggly; they had to be rivers. And I could see that many of these rivers ran into one another, connected, so that, starting in central New Jersey, where Phil and I lived, it looked like one might journey the sixty miles to Manhattan by water.

Many's the time I had, like millions of others, traveled to

Manhattan by train or bus or automobile. I wondered what it would be like to go there by a more exclusive, almost secret route.

Adventure is carrying out one's fantasies. A fantasy I have entertained since childhood, which I imagine many others share, is throwing a stick into a creek and following it along the banks of larger and larger waterways until it reaches the sea. I was reminded of this fantasy now not only by my map musings but by a book I had read to my children called *Paddle-to-the-Sea*. This is the story of a tiny canoe carved out of a block of wood by an American Indian child and placed atop a steep hillside in rural Minnesota. When the winter snows melt, "Paddle" floats on a rivulet down the hill into a creek, thence into a river, and finally into Lake Superior. Over many months, it travels through each of the Great Lakes, over Niagara Falls, through the Saint Lawrence Seaway, and, finally, to the ocean.

It seemed to me that one might carry my childhood fantasy and *Paddle-to-the-Sea* one step further. Instead of launching a surrogate stick or canoe, why not make such a trip oneself? Further, instead of a wilderness trip, why not urban waters? If my map was accurate, one could start in a creek near Phil's house and, following larger and larger waterways, make it to the Atlantic; thence up New York Harbor, past the Statue of Liberty and Ellis Island, to Manhattan. Perhaps no one had made this voyage since the American Indians. Maybe they never did it either.

And even if they did, such a trip would today have a political component it could not have had for the Native Americans. People in New York are afraid to come out in the streets. By canoeing into New York we would show them they had nothing to be afraid of. We would lift the siege on the town.

I told Phil this trip would make us famous. "There'll be fire-boats with streams of water in the sky, and the mayor will give us keys to the city, and they'll helicopter our women up there and give them corsages, and we'll make speeches on the steps of City Hall, and. . . ."

"Cut the crap," Phil interrupted. "If I come, it's for one reason:

your wife's too young to be a widow." Phil had four days off from the firehouse coming up almost immediately, and I had had the children entirely in my care for a week while Patricia was off at an American Bar Association convention in San Franciso, so she owed me. Phil and I made a deal: if I handled the arrangements, he would make the trip.

So, on a hot and humid August day, almost exactly a year since the canoe trip around Manhattan, I drove to Phil's house near Hightstown, New Jersey. His live-in girlfriend, Abigail, was there. "When are you going to go with *me* on one of these trips?" she was saying to Phil as I arrived. "I will, I will," Phil said. I busied myself with some of the gear, pretending not to hear.

"I'm serious," she said.

"I'm serious too," Phil said.

Abigail turned to me. "Michael," she said, "would *you* take me on one of your trips?"

I looked at Phil. "You mean Phil and you and me?" I said. "Sure."

"No," Abigail said. "I mean you and me. Phil won't take me."

I looked over at Phil again, uncomfortably. He rolled his eyes. I said, "Well, I would in theory."

"What do you mean, *in theory?*"

"Well," I said, "you're a pretty woman, Abigail."

"What's that got to do with it? Couldn't you go on an adventure with a woman and just be friends? Why couldn't you and I go on a trip just like you and Phil go on a trip?"

"We could. Like I said, *in theory.*"

Abigail shook her head in disgust. She was right, of course. I wish I *could* go on a trip with Abigail or another woman without the sexual question coming up. I wish I could have friendships with attractive women without thinking about sleeping with them. But I can't. Okay, so I'm a Neanderthal. I can't help it; that's the way I am.

Later, when we were alone, Phil said, "Women. They're all brain surgeons."

"Whatya mean?" I asked.

"We men; we're animals. We get mad, we hit somebody. Women don't hit. They operate on your brain."

"Like?"

"Like, you're thinking of going to a football game. You haven't bought the tickets yet, but you're thinking about it. Before you know it you're not going to that football game; you're in Macy's shopping for some goddam drapes, and you don't even know how you got there. Later, you figure it out: brain surgery."

At forty, Phil has never been married—there's been a succession of Abigails in his life. I've never known his girlfriends well because, by the time I started to know one, she was gone and another was in her place. Phil's always saying that he envies me my family, but he doesn't seem overeager to have one of his own. One of his favorite expressions is "pussy-whipped" or just "whipped" for short. Whenever we talk about a married guy Phil invariably says, "Yeah, well that guy's whipped." I don't know whether Phil thinks I'm whipped or not. Probably so.

One time we were talking about a mutual friend, and Phil said, "That is one sorry, pussy-whipped guy."

"Well," I said, "there's worse things to be whipped by."

Phil thought about that for a moment. Then he said, "Yeah, you're right." That's one thing about Phil. He's the most open-minded person I know, the most reasonable. If he thinks you have a point, he'll say so and not carry on an argument just to carry on an argument. Which is why I like to hang out with him. At the university, all people *do* is carry on arguments just to carry on arguments.

We carried Phil's now familiar yellow canoe out of his garage, down the street, past a Seven-Eleven, past the rescue squad, across a highway, and down to the bank of the Millstone River. We loaded the canoe with sleeping bags, a pup tent, and a plastic garbage bag full of easy-to-serve food I'd scraped from the supermarket shelves.

I told Phil I hadn't had time to get anything more elaborate, but the truth was I rather liked what I had picked out and my manner of purchasing it. I'd swept through the A & P with no list—so uncharacteristic of me—and bought whatever came to mind in a devil-may-care way. Besides the inevitable jar of Gooberjelly and some cans of sardines and boxes of raisins, prunes, and dried apricots, I had laid in a terrific supply of Hershey bars, sunflower seeds, Planters peanuts, pretzels, Mounds bars, and Cracker Jacks.

"Where're we going," Phil asked, "to a drive-in movie?"

"It's a balanced diet," I insisted, thinking maybe I should have made a list after all.

"Balanced with what?"

The Millstone was a tiny stream here, so narrow we could barely get our canoe into it. It was like putting a battleship into a ditch. In the first fifty yards our prow went up on the bank twice. The second time the stern swung around onto the opposite bank, and there we were, athwart the river, more bridge than boat.

"Steer, dammit," Phil groused.

A hundred yards farther on we hit the first of many snags. A tree had fallen across the river, and we had to portage around it. Soon after, we came to a place where the river seemed to stop altogether. There was a stick and mud obstruction, and we had to clamber over it to where the river oozed through on the other side.

"I forget. Is this trip by land or by water?" Phil asked, breathing hard.

The Leni-Lenape called the Millstone Matawang, which means hard to travel. Those Indians knew what they were talking about. The river moves through the flatlands of New Jersey with almost no current, so debris piles up everywhere. Scientists believe the Millstone may once have flowed in the opposite direction. Maybe so; it sure wasn't traveling with much energy in the direction we were going.

As the miles passed, the river widened and the snags abated. We hadn't seen anyone or anything since we started, but just ahead was Route 1, where trucks and cars roared by overhead, engulfed in fumes. Their drivers were intent on the road, didn't look toward the river, didn't see us. These people worked in New York and would be there in an hour. Phil's and my time schedule differed so radically from theirs that we could have been traveling through another dimension.

We entered a culvert that passed under the highway. It was cool and dark under there, and our voices bounced off the corrugated steel roof. As we emerged into sunlight, we could see the towers of Princeton University off in the distance and, just ahead, Lake Carnegie.

Carnegie is an artificial lake, made by damming the Millstone to form a racing course for the Princeton rowing team. It being summer, no one was on the lake, and, in the freedom of open water, we skimmed along its surface like Olympic oarsmen.

It was a simple portage around the dam, but on the bank a herd of Canada geese blocked us, hissing and giving off nasty looks. And I do mean herd, not flock; these geese were more like cattle than robins. Canada geese have all but taken over New Jersey in recent years. They don't fly south in winter or up to Canada in summer anymore, but have settled in New Jersey year-round— the greenhouse effect some say. These geese lumber about making a terrible nuisance of themselves, honking incessantly and covering the landscape with green turds.

The geese had surrounded us, and one now ran at Phil and nipped him on the ass. "Son of a bitch," Phil screamed, truly enraged. He ran at the herd full tilt, waving his arms. Honking indignantly, the geese glided swiftly down the muddy bank and, achieving liftoff, sped down the river between the overarching trees.

Below Lake Carnegie the Millstone has real current and even occasional white water. We began to pass little river towns, with their colonial architecture and "George Washington Slept Here" signs. "No wonder that guy became the father of our country," Phil said. "He slept everywhere."

Actually, I told Phil, father of our country or not, Washington was almost certainly sterile. Martha was a young widow with two children when George married her, but they had no children together. That was probably because Washington had had a near-fatal case of mumps at age thirteen. That'll make you sterile as effectively as a vasectomy.

Phil seemed impressed—as if this was a special kind of information to which only professors were privy. But then he said,

"Yeah, but how do we know George wasn't so busy sleeping elsewhere that he didn't have time for Martha?"

Farther along the Millstone we approached the yellow brick buildings of the almost hidden Pillar of Fire religious community, which more than once has been all but wiped out by the flooding river. Often, when driving at night, I had unwittingly picked up these evangelicals on my car radio screaming about Jesus. Now, in daylight, their silent campus looked like the setting for an episode of the *Twilight Zone*.

A mile farther on, the Raritan swept in from the west and the Millstone hurried to meet it, disappearing into it without a gurgle. The Raritan is New Jersey's longest river, running for a hundred miles. The Leni-Lenape called it Laletan, meaning smooth-running or gentle. It was both of these things, but two miles after entering it we experienced an exception. Coming around a bend, we heard the roar of water and, before we could stop, rocketed over a sloping obstruction in the river, bumped noisily, and continued on through the crashing water and foam. "What in hell was that?" Phil said.

We learned later that these obstructions are called weirs and were built to raise the level of the river at certain points to keep the Delaware and Raritan Canal, which parallels the Raritan at this point, well fed. A week after our trip a young man went over a weir just like ours and drowned when his canoe capsized and he was sucked under by the churning waters. It took divers two days to extricate his body.

The day was moving on, and dark clouds were making it look even later than it was. A storm was obviously on its way. Phil suggested that, instead of camping on the bank, we sleep in my office at Rutgers University. "On a canoe trip?" I said in disgust. I wanted to keep this trip pure. But when a bolt of lightning cut across the sky, immediately chased by explosive thunder, I said, "Okay, okay," and we pushed on toward New Brunswick.

Reaching Johnson & Johnson, world Band-Aid headquarters, we hauled our canoe up the right bank and stowed it in some bushes along the narrow strip of land between the river and the canal. Then we took a footbridge over the canal into the J & J compound. It was almost dark, the working day long over, as we walked past buildings and through deserted courtyards, looking for a way out. "Sing," Phil said.

"What?"

"Sing. If we sing the cops'll know we're not vandals, just stupid." Phil began to sing "Camptown Races," and I sheepishly joined in.

As we rounded the last building, loudly intoning "Doodah, doodah," we found ourselves facing a uniformed guard. He leaned on the doorjamb of a guardhouse just inside the main gate, eyeing us, a pistol on his hip. An eerie blue light flickered over his shoulder.

It came from inside the guardhouse. Peering inside, I saw ten closed-circuit television sets covering each area of the compound we had passed through. Our canoe's bow stuck up into the picture on the first set. Ever since leaving the river we had been under surveillance.

But the guard was friendly enough, especially when I told him I worked across the street at the university. He knew professors as eccentrics, capable of anything, even showing up by water at Johnson & Johnson's back door. He kindly offered to keep an eye on our canoe.

Phil and I passed out the J & J gate into downtown New Brunswick, carrying our sleeping bags, and had dinner at a place I knew on George Street called Tumulty's—best cheeseburgers in the world, and they come with a baked potato and hearts of lettuce and the sour cream and blue cheese are free. "Screw cholesterol," Phil said.

"You don't worry about cholesterol?" I asked.

"Nah, it's just something these nutritional fascists have cooked up. Next thing you know people are going to be keeling over for want of cholesterol or their bones cracking for lack of the grease that binds them together. You wait: pretty soon doctors'll be insisting we scarf down as much cholesterol as possible. They'll be prescribing cholesterol pills for most folks and giving it to the critical cases intravenously."

Stuffed, we walked to campus and my office in Ruth Adams

Hall. It was delicious fun using my office for a purpose so unlike what I'm usually there for, a bit like taking an abandoned church and turning it into an art gallery, a sort of adaptive reuse. I laid out our sleeping bags on the worn and slightly moldy carpet between my desk and the bookcases. Like a couple of teenagers at a slumber party, Phil and I talked in our bags for a long time before falling asleep.

"Aghhhhhhh!" Phil was screaming. "Aghhhhhhh!" someone else screamed as I fumbled in my pants pocket for my Swiss Army knife. The lights were on, and Phil was sitting up in his sleeping bag, pointing at the janitor who was standing by the light switch, pointing at him. The janitor had come into my office to get the wastepaper basket, and he and Phil simultaneously terrorized each other. Suffice it to say it was some time before we got back to sleep.

At two in the morning, we were awakened again, this time by the rain and wind. My window sashes rattled like they were going to snap, and we could hear things crashing about outside. The clock radio I keep on my desk was full of news of a hurricane. "Naturally, you checked the weather report before we started?" Phil asked.

"Naturally," I replied.

There was a crack and then a thump as a tree went over outside and fell against the far corner of Ruth Adams Hall. "Jesus," Phil said.

By morning the storm had let up considerably, but it was still raining hard. We sat around in our sleeping bags trying to decide what to do. The radio predicted clearing by noon followed by high winds. Small craft warnings were in effect for the next two days. "Man, there is *no* craft smaller than ours," Phil said.

I made coffee with the meager fixings in the office. The cups were moldy, the instant coffee and Cremora stale, and ants were in the sugar bowl. I scribbled a note about it and tossed it in the To Do box on my desk. By eight o'clock the sun had come out, so we walked down George Street and had breakfast in

McDonald's. It began raining again just as we finished our Egg McMuffins, but we could wait no longer. Sprinting through Johnson & Johnson to the river, we dumped the water out of the canoe and, under a sodden sky, put out into the Raritan. It was a big, wide river now, tidal and swollen by the storm. The wind blew salt spray in our faces. It started raining harder, and I wished we had stayed longer at McDonald's. The sky turned an eerie shade of green, and then a solid, gray wall of rain moved up the river toward us. Before it hit, hailstones panged off the aluminum, and then it was on us and the canoe began to fill so fast we had to stop and bail. Our gear, stowed in plastic garbage bags, floated crazily about the canoe.

As quickly as it had arrived, the great wall continued upriver and the sun came out, this time for good. Steam rose from the back of Phil's T-shirt.

Downriver, a father and son appeared on the bank and began crabbing. We paused to watch them. They'd lower a chicken neck tied to a long string and, when a blue crab grabbed hold, gently drew him out of the water, still munching contentedly on the neck.

Ahead was the New Jersey Turnpike, twelve lanes of steel and concrete and burning rubber, twenty with the shoulders. We entered the long darkness beneath that highway, the widest in the world, but except for the muffled sounds of the traffic whirring above us and the echo of our paddling rebounding from the bridge supports, it was quiet and cool under there. Smoothly, we steered toward the light.

We emerged into a new world. The Raritan, which had been straight upriver, now began to snake in great curves toward the coast. The current slowed to nothing, and we could feel the tide moving against us. The going got slower and slower as a vast salt marsh closed around us, reeds as far as the eye could see. Channels went off in all directions, and at times we thought we were lost. Then a huge tank with the words "Gas Cools Too" rose up behind us, while out toward the coast a power plant put out great funnels of smoke. As long as these landmarks were in sight, we knew which direction to head. And as one grew larger, the other smaller, we made progress.

But the going was agonizingly slow. "Naturally, you checked the tide charts before we left?" Phil asked.

"Natch," I replied, silently cursing myself for having imagined the tides wouldn't be as critical as on our trip around Manhattan. Now I knew: tides are always critical. Whenever we stopped paddling momentarily, we were driven upriver. Why didn't the ocean stay where it was and stop coming up the river?! Exhausted, we tied on to a wooden pile that stood in the reeds, rested our backs, and ate our lunch. With no solid land around, we took turns peeing off the ends of the rocking canoe—an act of extreme delicacy and grace if it's to be accomplished without mishap.

We untied and continued paddling east toward the sea, every foot forward a struggle. I counted reeds. When I got to a hundred, I started over again.

An hour dragged by before we reached the power plant. Now we began laboriously paddling toward the dim outline of the Garden State Parkway bridge. It took us another hour to reach it, but now we knew the coast couldn't be far. We passed under several more bridges and came alongside the city of Perth Amboy. Threading our way through the tethered boats of the Perth Amboy Yacht Club, we entered Raritan Bay.

Fog was rolling in. A tanker, sounding its horn, moved past us up the channel of water between New Jersey and Staten Island called the Arthur Kill. We turned left, following the tanker, letting it run interference for us. By now the gloom was complete in the kill, regularly the scene of spectacular oil spills, chemical explosions, and collisions. Phil said, "Let's get out of here before we get run over."

We searched for a place to land. The New Jersey side was nothing but tank farms and chemical plants—not a healthy place to camp. On the Staten Island side, a short distance up the kill, there appeared to be a beach, so we steered for it, getting there just as the last of the light was eclipsed by the fog and the night.

In the glow of our flashlights, we saw that this beach was just as uninviting as anything could have been on the Jersey side. At water's edge was the wreck of a burned pier, while the sand was littered with the better part of a Formica kitchen set, stacks of beer bottles, orange peels, light bulbs, tires, plastic jugs, shoes— even someone's dirty jockey shorts. I nearly stepped on a dead cat, its teeth snarling defiance even now. Battalions of dark green horseshoe crabs crept over the garbage-strewn sand, and the beach was pocked with deep holes, as if it had recently been bombed. Finding the cleanest place available, we pitched the pup tent and laid out the sleeping bags. Phil spotted neon lights flickering off in the distance. "Forget the Cracker Jacks," he said. "Let's get a real supper."

We had landed at Tottenville, a small town on the tip of Staten Island, which, because of its isolation, seems an unlikely part of New York City. Coming up off that ghastly beach, we walked down a weed-filled street to a place called Dave's Bar, where we ordered beers and scanned the meager menu.

On the next stool was a retired dockworker named Smiley who told us he once worked on the destroyed pier down at the beach when it was the New Jersey ferry slip. The ferry had been replaced by the Outerbridge Crossing bridge just upriver. Smiley was blind drunk. "Where you boys staying?" he kept asking us, and when we told him it didn't seem to register because a few minutes later he would ask, "Where you boys staying?" and we would tell him and he would ask again. Finally he got it, because this conspiratorial look came into his eyes and he whispered huskily, "Watch out for the water rats."

"Zip that tent up tight," Phil said after we returned to the beach. Tired as I was, I sat up a long time in my sleeping bag, wondering whether water rats bite through nylon. As I stared out at the dark Arthur Kill, a giant tanker slid by, the *Jaime Menéndez,* no doubt bound for Venezuela.

———————————

We awoke to a flapping tent and what sounded like a gale outside. As we sat on a beached telephone pole, munching our breakfast of Pop Tarts and prunes, I realized the wind was blowing from the north, the direction we were headed. The current would also be against us in the kill, and, if this weren't enough, I figured by the clock that the tides would soon be going out.

We got into the water and began struggling up the kill. It was like paddling on a treadmill. We fought the water, biting off short distances and then resting, tied to a pipe or stick onshore so as not to slip backward. "This sure isn't like Huck and Jim," Phil shouted over the wind. "This sure isn't going with the flow."

"Maybe that's good," I replied. "Going with the flow got Huck and Jim deeper and deeper into slave territory."

This was a rationalization, I knew, but there was an element of seriousness in what I had said. America has always gone with the flow, taken the easiest path, avoided facing its problems. Maybe Phil and I, paddling against wind and current and tide, represented a new way of looking at the country. Or so I told myself as I sweated and ached and groaned.

Slowly we approached Fresh Kills, the largest garbage dump in the world, reputedly one of only two structures created by humans that can be seen with the unaided eye from space—the other being the Great Wall of China. Fresh Kills is forty stories high, several miles long, and smells. It was as if garbage were being mined elsewhere—Brooklyn, Queens, Manhattan—and they were stockpiling it on Staten Island. Phil began loudly singing Woody Guthrie's song "This Land Is Your Land." In the eternal struggle between the land and the sea, this was one place where the land, an alien land, was winning the battle.

The dump finally behind us, we passed among the rusting hulks of a graveyard of ferry boats anchored in the kill just off the Staten Island shore. This was where they mothballed New York's ferries when they were replaced by bridges and tunnels. You could still make out the names through the rust: the *Sarah Jane,* the *Lackawanna Chief,* the *Blarney Stone,* the *Captain Stokes.* A German shepherd guard dog, barking insanely as he jumped from boat to boat trying to get at us, completed the melancholy scene.

Just past the ferry graveyard the tide and wind intensified, and our forward progress became one long slow-motion movie. We got out and tried pulling the canoe along the shore, but it kept floating in and smacking against the rocky bank. We tried it with me in the canoe ruddering, Phil on the shore grumbling, "I don't exactly dig this *African Queen* shit," and made a mile or so this way when, at a little inlet, Phil stepped into the cold, toxic water up to his neck. "There goes my chance of having children," Phil said.

"Like G. W.?" I replied.

"He didn't need children to prove *his* manhood," Phil said. "They gave him the Washington Monument. I bet they buried the sucker under there on his back."

I made a fire on the bank out of some orange crates and toasted Phil's clothes on a stick. He crouched naked on his haunches on the scurvy bank, acknowledging the jeers from a passing tugboat by mooning its crew with his very white and hairy ass. When Phil's clothes were dry, we tried paddling again and, after another mile, reached a Mobil tanker-cleaning plant. As we rested, tied to a wooden pile, a voice called from above, "You want some coffee?"

Gratefully, we climbed an iron ladder into a maze of pipes and valves and were led into a low building full of hissing steam. The coffee tasted marvelous, and there was Danish too. Our grease-covered benefactor had an idea: "Why don't you get a tow?" he suggested, offering the materials for a crude sign.

"Uh uh," I said. "We wouldn't be getting there on our own power."

But Phil leaped at the notion. "You compulsive nut," he said. "We'd have gotten there on our own power long ago if you'd paid some attention to the tides." Phil was on the floor at once, scraping away with chalk at a huge hunk of tar paper. Then he stood, proudly displaying his artwork. "Tow up River," it said.

Back in the Arthur Kill, we waved the sign at a succession of tugboats. Dropping the sign to let a tanker pass, we hoisted it again when a powerboat puttered up the kill. It accelerated when it spotted us, its occupants laughing as we almost swamped in their wake.

Then a large yacht came along, churning up water. Phil waved the sign while I wigwagged my paddle. Two men stood on the bridge wearing wraparound sunglasses, impassive. They looked like mobsters. One of them motioned for us to throw him our bow rope, tied it to a cleat, and the motors exploded.

The canoe leaped forward with a violent jerk. Phil was thrown off the front seat into the bottom of the canoe. I nearly went overboard backward, recovered, and eased myself down behind Phil. Just over the mountain of water that had risen in front of us I made out the improbable name of the boat: *Melancholy Baby.*

Now the canoe mounted the boat's huge wake and began to dance on its crest, some fifteen feet in the air. All we could do was grasp the gunwales and hang on. We passed the tugboats that had gone by earlier, and their wakes slapped against ours, destabilizing it and sending us still higher. We passed the powerboat whose occupants had taunted us, and Phil joyously gave them the finger. We were now so high we were actually looking down on the bridge of *Melancholy Baby.* "Let us buy you beers later," Phil shouted to our benefactors.

Over the sound of the motors and rushing water they were bound to misunderstand. One of the men descended into the cabin and came out with several beers. Before we could stop him, cans were rocketing toward us like cannonballs. The first nearly took off Phil's head. "No," we both yelled, but the guy pitched another that hit the side of the canoe with a rasping noise that sounded like the aluminum had been pierced. Any moment I expected the water to rush in.

Phil made a brilliant catch of the next can, and I caught the following one with my left hand. The man seemed to be asking if we wanted more. "No," we mouthed, hoping he could read our lips. With relief we watched him return to the bridge. Our beers were so agitated by flight they exploded as we opened them and foamed down our faces, but it didn't matter. Nothing mattered besides the surprising fact that we were still alive.

Now we were speeding through the industries that line the Arthur Kill. Besides the refineries and chemical plants, there were huge rock-crushing mills, auto junkyards, sewage treatment plants. We passed the Staten Island site where fifty-two men died while welding the seams of a supposedly empty giant gas tank that had gas trapped between its outer and inner skins. I pointed at the remains of the wretched tank, as big as a football stadium, and Phil said, "No wonder they call this the Arthur *Kill.*"

We passed under the Goethals Bridge and, at the top of Staten Island, turned right into the Kill Van Kull, the passage between Newark and New York harbors. Bumper-to-bumper in there with tugboats, water boiling around us, we charged under the great arch of the Bayonne Bridge.

Near the northeastern tip of Staten Island, *Melancholy Baby* veered to the right and cast us off. We tried to thank our benefactors for the tow, but they disappeared without a backward glance behind great volumes of water. Now we sat rocking in their waves, poised to dash between the ships emerging from the Kill Van Kull. It was like crossing a wide highway on foot; you wait until nothing is coming and then run like hell. After a freighter passed, Phil yelled, "Let's go," and we dug in and dashed across the last of the kill.

Now we were alone in the vast basin of New York Harbor, our canoe a yellow spot in a world of blue. Overhead, jets streamed toward Kennedy Airport, and to our right the Staten Island ferry plowed toward the Battery. The twin towers of the World Trade Center were far up the harbor, clean and geometrical.

We paddled from wave to wave, moving forward at unaccustomed speed. For once, the tide was going our way, and we rolled toward Manhattan as if a powerful motor was attached to our stern. The Statue of Liberty was just ahead, immense from our vantage point low down in the canoe, its eyes oracular, its stance almost menacing.

Beyond the statue was Ellis Island, then in the early stages of restoration. But it was after hours and the workers were gone, so Phil and I sneaked onto the island, ignoring the No Trespassing signs that covered the seawall. We landed next to an old, high-chimneyed ferryboat that quietly rotted at a collapsed dock.

The heavy, ornate buildings of Ellis Island recalled Eastern Europe—wrecked, but still exuding the little discourtesies of bureaucrats past. Wooden water towers perched precariously on ruined copper roofs. Doors were ajar, so we were free to explore the crumbling interiors of the buildings. In the Great Hall, where sixteen million immigrants were processed over forty years, Phil and I shouted to each other across the cavernous space, our voices echoing. "No Micks need apply," I yelled to Phil, to which he responded, "Why don't you Jewboys go back where you came from?"

Later, Phil asked, "Where'd you ever get a WASP name like Rockland anyway?" and I told him that my name originated right here, on Ellis Island, perhaps in this very room. My grandfather had been assigned the name by an immigrant inspector who gave up trying to pronounce his real name, which resembled Rockland—Reichland or something like that. To this day I do not know what my last name, a casualty of the melting pot, should have been.

As we wandered through the buildings we happened upon a printing plant rusting in place, a morgue with pulled-out body shelves on rollers, a ruined chapel where the plaster hung down in festoons and mildewed hymnals littered the scratched wooden floor. There were old iron beds everywhere and record files strewn about. The windows of most of the buildings were broken, and birds of all kinds fluttered about. A squadron of pigeons clattered toward us, veering off at the last moment and rising to their nests high in the cornices.

Night was coming on, and there were no lights in the buildings. We stumbled outside and, with the moon's assistance, pitched our tent in a sunken soccer field where the immigrants must have played while waiting to be processed. The goalposts had long ago rotted and fallen over into the tall weeds at the edge of the field, where we found them with bits of flaking white paint still clinging to the wood. We sat in the field and ate our remaining food and looked at the city in front of us.

Lights were coming on all over Manhattan, whole buildings springing to life. The towers of the city looked so close you could touch them, yet they seemed unreal, painted on a huge, shimmering canvas. Upriver were the dark forms of the New Jersey Palisades. Everything we could see was ours, belonged exclusively to us. "This is the most beautiful sight I've ever seen," Phil said, uncharacteristically emotional.

It was a magical time. In the middle of the world's greatest city, we were totally alone. There was only an owl up in one of the ailanthus trees that proliferate on Ellis Island, growing out of every crack, even out of the wrecked roofs of the buildings. The owl left its perch and circled time after time, glaring down at us. Finally, it swooped off toward New Jersey, ceding its island home to us for the night.

We got up early the next morning so as to be off Ellis before the construction crews showed up. The water was still black, but the sun peeked through the crack between the World Trade Center towers. The city looked sparkling and clean as we paddled across the water to the Battery.

Manhattan wasn't awake yet. Perhaps this is why there were no fireboats shooting streams of water into the sky and no keys to the city, no helicopters, no mayor and crowds to greet us, no corsages for our women, no women, not even any of the fearful citizens we had come to liberate.

But after hauling the canoe up the face of the seawall into Battery Park, we *were* greeted by a homeless man on a bench. Incredibly, he was the same homeless man, on the same bench, we had met when we canoed around Manhattan a year before. He was just coming awake. He sat up and stared at us, his eyes widening. "Say," he said, aren't you. . . ?"

"Yeah," Phil said.

"Well, well, well," the homeless guy, said, shaking his head. "But where. . . ?

"China," Phil said.

PART TWO

THE GARDEN STATE

Zen and the Art
of Biking Route 1

That concrete whizzing by five inches below
your foot. . . . You can put your foot down
and touch it anytime.

ROBERT M. PIRSIG, *ZEN AND THE ART OF*
MOTORCYCLE MAINTENANCE

A few months after the canoe trip to New York, I turned to my
own New Jersey. If adventure in the city intrigued me, so did
adventure in that strange borderland of the built environment
where city and country collide: the suburbs.

New Jersey is the most suburban state in the country. Its sprawl-
ing suburbs so overpower its poor, abandoned cities you could
almost say that they *are* its cities. These suburbs are so built up
that, in many areas, one town flows directly into the next, with
no open land between them nor frontier landmarks more remarkable than a bowling alley or a pizzeria. New Jersey is the most
densely populated state in the nation, more densely populated
than India.

In a sense, New Jersey is one big city, yet it continues to
pretend that it is rural, calls itself the Garden State. Our land is
toxic, but we imagine ourselves as living in a garden, in purest
nature, in Eden. We even paint the crushed-rock hillsides of the
Garden State Parkway green.

If New Jersey is like a city, it still has its "parks"—its mountains and beaches. Yet, it is small enough to embrace. The governor helicopters about the state in minutes, and the citizenry can
motor almost anywhere in New Jersey in a couple of hours—

a fact that prompts fantasies in people like me of crossing the state by other means. I had already canoed across much of New Jersey on the way to Manhattan. I thought: Why not cross it this time by bike?

When I began my trip that Saturday morning, Trenton was just across the Delaware River, the gold dome of the state capitol reflecting the rich autumn light. My bike leaned on its kickstand as I checked the bag containing tools and extra socks and liniment and toothbrush and candy bars to make sure it was fastened securely to the rear rack. Tire pressure was all right, brakes firm. Okay, so the fingerless racing gloves were an affectation; they made me feel good.

I got on the bike and began pedaling across the bridge on the pedestrian walkway. I had started at the state line, midway across the bridge to Pennsylvania, so that no one could say I hadn't done all of Route 1 in New Jersey—though I'm not sure who, besides myself, would worry about such a thing.

As I entered Trenton, Route 1 disappeared into the city streets, so I had to follow signs carefully. Left turn. Right turn. Past the State Street Mall, past the monument to George Washington, past the not yet awake, debris-littered ghetto. Soon, a little strip mall—with a Burger King, a pool supply store, a car wash, a dry cleaners, a Modern Mattress store, a frame shop—announced the beginning of the suburbs. I angled out toward Brunswick Circle.

It was then I first experienced the heady craziness of being on a bicycle in a place meant for automobiles. Going around the circle, with cars honking furiously at me, I saw that, if I was going to survive this trip, I would have to insist on the integrity of the space I was occupying. That was the challenge: to construct a corridor of calm through New Jersey, from Trenton to the George Washington Bridge, from the Delaware to the Hudson—and to do it on Route 1, perhaps the busiest highway in America.

If you're looking for the real New Jersey, try Route 1. It goes through every town and city it can. When people want to go shopping or see a movie, they head for Route 1. When truck drivers want decent food, they get off the Jersey Turnpike and find a diner on Route 1. There's a thriving weekly newspaper called *Route One,* there's a comic book whose truck driver hero goes by the handle "U.S. 1," and there's even a poets' cooperative in central New Jersey that calls itself U.S. 1. "Route 1," says one of the poets, "*is* New Jersey."

Route 1 is also the first national highway. Traveling west, you cross one by one the other north-south, odd-numbered national roads until you reach Route 101 on the Pacific Coast. Route 1 is the granddaddy of these roads. Some sections of it follow one-time American Indian trails, while others bear historic names. In Pennsylvania, Route 1 is the Lincoln Highway. In the Bronx, a piece of Route 1 hooks around under the IRT elevated train and heads north as the Boston Post Road. Farther north, Paul Revere used this same Boston Post Road for his famous ride.

In the 1930s, Route 1 was still sufficiently rural that the Federal Writers' Project recommended traveling it as a vacation. Their book on Route 1 is full of tourist tidbits to check out along the way: a house beside the road in Maine where Marie Antoinette's friends intended to hide her if she hadn't been beheaded; the goats grazing at Standard Oil's New Jersey Route 1 refinery, replacing mechanical lawn mowers and their dangerous sparks. The fascination with Route 1 continues in a recently published book, *U.S. 1: America's Original Main Street.*

I used to go to work on Route 1. The stretch I took every day was only twelve miles long, but I drove well over 100,000 miles on it over the years. That's four times around the world. I wore out an automobile just on that twelve-mile stretch of Route 1.

I got to where I knew every rundown gas station and motel and roadhouse bar and grill along that stretch and even some of the lonely-looking people who lived beside the highway. There was this fat lady I'd see just about every day walking along the shoulder from the mobile-home park to the Seven-Eleven to get her newspaper and a quart of milk. Eventually we got to where we'd wave. When I'd approach the section of road where she lived, I'd find myself uncontrollably singing that old song that begins, "I don't want her / you can have her / she's too fat for me."

Guiltily, I'd try to stop; you're not supposed to sing songs like that anymore, and besides I increasingly felt a certain loyalty to that lady and thought I oughtn't to be singing a song she wouldn't like. But next day, as I was approaching the mobile-home park, I'd start singing it all over again, in my head if not with my voice, sometimes to the point of extreme irritation.

If you spend a lot of time on a highway, you wonder what's beyond the section you drive. Before I ever thought of biking Route 1 through New Jersey, I fantasized biking it from the Canadian border all the way to the Florida Keys. I've heard of a sign at water's edge in Key West, nothing beyond there but Cuba, that says, "This is the end of Route 1." Maybe I'll make that trip someday and have a look at that sign.

Fantasies of trips are real important to me. If I learned I had a short time to live, I would definitely do that Route 1 bike trip from Canada to Florida. Maybe I think I'd be cheating death that way; as long as I was moving I couldn't die. But mainly it would be a way to go out in style. I'd be saying, "Dying's not so bad"—and maybe even believing it. People wouldn't be gathered around my deathbed, feeling sorry for me; they'd hear that I'd keeled over on the road somewhere near the end of Route 1. I'd be like an American Indian going alone to the mountaintop, saying, "This is a good day to die."

Lest I give the impression I'm some kind of superjock biking pro, with leather helmet and black stretch shorts, I should say that I bike in jeans and sneakers and a windbreaker and that, before doing the New Jersey segment of Route 1, I hadn't biked much more than around the corner to get a half gallon of milk. I had a rusty old bike with no gears and just a foot brake. All I knew was that pumping the pedals made the wheels go round.

While I was considering the Route 1 trip, the bike store in my town announced a terrific sale. So I traded my old Schwinn for a Raleigh Gran Prix—a little like exchanging a battered Chevy for a new Ferrari; one speed to ten overnight. The Gran Prix was built like a gazelle and had hand brakes and gears and these weird-looking mechanisms called derailleurs that amble about like gyroscopes, moving the chain from one big-toothed gear to another. And the chain wasn't your normal bike chain. It looped around through the derailleurs like a liquid pretzel.

The Gran Prix was a gorgeous machine. I was determined not only to ride it but to know it intimately, but I was so afraid of breaking something that the bike sat in the garage two months without my once getting on it. By that time most of the air had gone out of the tires.

I read in the paper that the local adult school was offering a five-night bike maintenance course, so I put some air in the tires, got on the Gran Prix for the first time, and rode it over to the high school. If something went wrong on the way over, my instructor would be able to fix it.

The course was a nightmare. The instructor would circle the room selecting bikes for demonstration purposes. "No, not mine," I wanted to scream, "do it to his." The last night of the course the instructor stripped my bike down to nuts and bolts and told me to put it together while the whole class watched. I anticipated leaving that night with the Gran Prix in a shopping basket, but I reconstructed it somehow and proudly rode it home.

The course proved useful shortly into the Route 1 trip. Coming along the highway shoulder just north of Trenton, I was distracted by a tiny ranch house incongruously stuck between two malls that sported a sign reading "Mrs. Miller's Horoscope Readings." I hit some sand, the front wheel jackknifed, and I nearly flew over the handlebars. When I tried to pedal again there was this awful grinding noise and the bike wouldn't move. The liquid pretzel had fallen off.

I paced the side of the highway, berating myself for my carelessness and cursing the delicacy of the Gran Prix and its fussy European pretensions. This had never happened with my trusty American Schwinn, perhaps because nothing could fall off the Schwinn; it was quite nicely rusted in place. I was so desperate I found myself wondering: Would the bike store take the expensive Gran Prix back for the battered Schwinn, even trade?

Calm down, I said to myself. Remembering the course at the

adult school, I realized all I had to do was lower the rear derailleur and ease the chain back onto the sprockets. Piece of cake. I cut my finger doing it, and scratched some paint off the bike, but I didn't care. As I wiped the blood and grease off on a telephone pole, I felt as if, simultaneously, the Gran Prix and I had lost our virginity. We could handle anything now.

I began to settle into the trip. The trick was to keep up a steady pace, not too fast downhill, not too slow up. That way you got just so tired, no more, and the miles went by. I wanted to make as many miles as possible that first day; the traffic was bound to get worse the farther north I went.

I had now entered that twelve-mile section of Route 1 I took to work every day. It looked different from the bike. First, I was traveling more like six than sixty. Also, I was actually *in* the landscape rather than just looking at it. Every colored leaf by the side of the road, every pebble, every piece of litter was significant. Biking is the right speed. You're going fast enough to get somewhere, but you don't miss anything along the way.

But traveling familiar terrain by a novel means can be strange. I passed the mobile-home park, and, just up the road on the shoulder, there was the fat lady returning from the store. I smiled and waved as I approached her, but she must have taken me for a weirdo or a pervert or had learned somehow about me singing that song, because she ignored me. Nah, it couldn't have been the song. I think she knew me only as the guy in the car, and since I wasn't in the car just then I couldn't be the guy. That proved to be correct. On the way to work the next Monday morning, I passed her in my car and she waved.

I passed the giant Quaker Bridge Mall and one corporate headquarters after another, their wall-to-wall carpets of perfect grass laid right to the highway's edge. Route 1 passed over the Millstone River, where Phil and I had canoed not long before on our way to New York. Two miles to the west stood Princeton University, looking like a European cathedral town—distant, removed from the noise and traffic of Route 1.

Up ahead, on the top of Sand Hill, was a small diner. Chaining my bike to a lamppost, I went in. The waitresses and customers all seemed to know one another. Behind the counter stood a tall cook with an enormous gut pushing out his T-shirt, tattoos on each arm, all the color steamed out of his face. I asked for pancakes.

"Why not?" he said.

I said something about being afraid that by two o'clock the breakfast menu was discontinued.

"You want pancakes, you get pancakes," he said.

I decided to live it up and asked if he had blueberry pancakes.

"Look buddy," he said, leaning on the counter with his face in mine, "you said pancakes. You didn't say blueberry pancakes. Whadya think this is, Howard Johnson's?"

But he didn't intend it mean. He and everyone at the counter broke into laughter, and soon I joined in and the cook smacked me on the shoulder. This is the insult-the-customer style of some Jersey diners.

A newspaper lay on the counter. "Three Balloonists Die in Mishap," the headline said. Why is it every time I go on a trip there's a colossal accident somewhere the day before? It's gotten to where if I go on a trip and there *isn't* an accident in the paper the day before, I worry. I figure it's my turn.

The burly trucker sitting next to me picking his teeth wasn't reassuring. He asked where I was going on the bike, and when I told him, he said, "You crazy or something? If my truck hit you on that bike you wouldn't even have fingerprints left."

I thanked him for the advice, but he persisted. "You watch out for the junkies when you pedal through Newark and Elizabeth. Those boys'll lift you off your bike, hit you over the head, and hock your bike before your legs stop turning. If they can get something for you, they'll hock you too."

Feeling shaky, I got back on the highway. Soon I was passing the New Jersey Dental Association, with the giant anodized tooth sculpture out front and the improbable address, One Dental Plaza. Pure New Jersey. In the middle of nowhere, by the side of Route 1: One Dental Plaza.

I was close to New Brunswick now. There were signs for Rutgers University, and I thought how nice it would be to get off the highway for a bit and go to my office the way Phil Herbert and I had done during the canoe trip to New York. My department had recently laid in fresh supplies, and I thought of what a pleasure it would be to make myself a cup of Earl Grey tea and go through the mail. But the sun was getting low. There wasn't time.

I crossed the Raritan River on the high bridge. On the other side, a large sign announced: "Adult Trading Post. Films Novelties Leathergoods." That's just what my aching body needed, some leathergoods! Actually, I wouldn't have minded the distractions of that roadside porn palace just then, but you can't skulk into such places on a bike the way you can in a car; you'd attract too much attention.

And this was near the university. What if one of the other professors saw me? I could just imagine a certain professor in the English Department, who lives nearby, saying, "Hey, Michael, wasn't that you I saw pedaling up to the Adult Trading Post on Route 1?" This guy is likely to serve on my promotion committee, and I think he already considers me not sufficiently scholarly. He once told me he found these trips of mine "amusing."

And then there were the students to consider. They imagine professors having no life whatsoever outside their classrooms and offices. When I encounter students of mine in places as innocent as alongside the canned soups in the A & P, they get this stricken look on their faces. "My God," they seem to be thinking, "he eats!" Imagine what a student would think seeing me enter the sinful precincts of the Adult Trading Post or, even worse, coming upon me in the dark among the peep machine booths.

So I kept going. Just ahead was S & M Auto Repair, unrelated. They had a car out front on its roof and a sign next to it saying, "Does your car turn over in the morning?"

Route 1 on the garish north side of the Raritan River was entirely a technological landscape of high-power lines, factories, and auto repair shops, with no trees that might have softened the view and, with their colors, reminded one of the season. It was also distinguished by the lack of any shoulder to ride on. I was in trouble here, the traffic thicker and nastier. I stayed as far over to the right as possible, putting out powerful vibes of invulnerability and pretending there was a force field around me right out of superhero comics. The right breathing, attuning my rhythms to those of the traffic, being consistent—I needed all of that to make it.

I passed through Edison and Metuchen. Route 9 came in from the coast to join Route 1, and now the traffic leaped still further upward in volume. I huddled down in my imaginary protective shield and concentrated on survival. Sure it was possible someone would hit me; but I could increase the danger by carelessness—by swerving out at an inopportune time or not watching for the occasional hubcap or muffler gathered by the curb.

It was getting dark, and all the care in the world wouldn't save me if I didn't stop soon for the night. I came to Woodbridge and a string of motels. One said, "Reasonable Rates," so I pulled up the bike on the ratty porch and walked into the office. "I'd like a room," I said.

"For how long?" the bored woman behind the desk asked.

"How long?"

"Two hours, four hours, or all night? Mirrored ceiling or plain? Waterbed or regular?"

"I'm just here to sleep," I said.

She didn't seem to hear me. "What's your license plate number?" she asked.

"I don't have a car," I said.

"I have to put down your plate number. State law," she said.

"I biked here," I said. She looked at me strangely. "I hope you don't mind if I bring the bike into my room."

She continued to stare at me. "We've never allowed bikes in our rooms before."

"Well, is there someone you can check with?" I asked. "I'll just stand it up in the corner of my room on its kickstand. It won't hurt anything."

Her expression indicated her strong preference that I immediately return to the highway and continue on my way so she wouldn't have to deal with me further. She sighed. Reluctantly, looking up at me meaningfully after marking each number, she dialed her black rotary phone. There was a long pause during which the woman stared at me and I fidgeted. Then she said into the receiver, "There's a fellow here wants to bring a bike. . . ."

Pause. Male squawking noises coming from the other end of the line.

"I said a bike."

Pause. Squawking noises, etc.

"A bike."

Pause. Squawking, etc.

"That's right. He wants to bring a bike into his room."

Pause. The party on the other end of the line now squawked uninterruptedly for several minutes. Occasionally, I would pick out the word *bike* in his conversation; otherwise, I couldn't hear what he said. Was he relating the history of the bicycle? Was he speculating on the percentage of the population that rides bikes? Perhaps he was considering whether to charge me for a double instead of a single because of the bike.

Blessedly, this conversation finally ended. "Sign here," the woman said, with an air suggesting the magnitude of the management's concession. I took my key and headed out the office door, feeling her eyes on my back. She must have been mad to know the kinky things I planned with my bike once I had it safely in my room.

But gluttony was the only vice I entertained at that moment, for I was starving. Up the highway was a diner I had passed just before arriving at the motel. It was one of those fancy ones, modern, with no counter. They even had hostesses to seat you. No matter: I had a steerburger deluxe, french fries, salad, and a chocolate milk shake.

Back at the motel, I read for a while and then decided to watch some television. There was a large sign on top of the set: "Warning: This television set is protected by a central burglar alarm system. Disconnection of the antenna, unplugging or lifting of the set will automatically activate the alarm. The Management." I turned the set on as gingerly as I could, cautious not to jiggle anything.

About to turn out the light, I realized I was still hungry. I had eaten just two hours before, but I put my clothes back on, walked to the diner, and had dinner all over again. The same hostess was on duty, but she didn't seem to recognize me.

——————

Waking Sunday morning, I jumped into my clothes and rode out onto Route 1. Traffic was light this early in the day, and I wanted to make some miles before stopping for breakfast. A strong breeze was blowing from the south, providing a nice tailwind.

After a half hour I stopped at a traditional railroad car diner. I sat at the counter and ordered the special: three eggs any style, choice of ham, bacon, or sausage, home fries, choice of toast or English muffin, juice, and as much coffee as I wanted, all for $1.99.

Back on the bike, I passed through Rahway, Linden, Elizabeth. There was still no shoulder, but that wasn't what scared me most. It was the drains. Storm drains appeared every fifty yards along the curb, with long, parallel steel grooves just slightly wider than my thin tires. Once my front wheel entered a groove there was no way out; I had to hang on, hoping to reach the other end without falling off or bending my front wheel. Approaching each drain I'd glance behind me and, if no vehicle was coming, would gratefully swerve around the drain.

The exits and jug handles were also dangerous. Cars cut in front of me at top speed. I learned to check if anyone behind me was preparing to turn off the highway at these places and, if not, would then race across the no-man's-land.

After the trip I read in the *New York Times* about a biker who was hit by an automobile that cut in front of him at a New Jersey jug handle. He had earlier made a worldwide bicycle tour without mishap.

I learned never to rely on motorists for my safety. Once a truck driver made me jump when he blew his air horn gratuitously, and a car full of teenagers yelled, "Get off the highway, dork!" but usually motorists weren't nasty, just oblivious. Their eyes registered the occasional pedestrian, and they certainly saw other vehicles, especially ones their own size or larger. But I was an anomaly, an in-between thing, neither fish nor fowl. They just didn't see me.

Surprisingly, I became more secure near Newark. Although traffic was heavier still, there was now a wide shoulder, the first since New Brunswick. I could even afford to look around me: at the Newark skyline; at the planes taking off from Newark Airport; at the silver towers of the World Trade Center over in Manhattan. I was riding high and feeling good.

Just ahead Route 1 split. I stopped and looked at the Sunoco road map I was carrying to see what was the best route from Newark over to Jersey City. The main branch of Route 1 crosses the North Jersey swamps on the black, ominous-looking Pulaski Skyway. From where I stood, the Pulaski looked like it had no shoulder or breakdown lane, and it was walled, so drivers would feel hemmed in and edgy. The Pulaski was too risky; I decided to take Alternate Route 1, the truck route.

Luckily, the bridge over the Passaic River had a walkway I could ride on, and so did the bridge crossing the much wider Hackensack. Below the Hackensack bridge tugboats steamed and magnetic cranes loaded barges with compacted automobiles. Not watching where I was going, I nearly collided with a Port-O-San outhouse that inexplicably blocked the walkway. I decided to use that Port-O-San; they owed me. Besides, no urban adventurer ever passes up an opportunity for a legitimate piss.

On the other side of the Hackensack was Jersey City. I pedaled through the city streets, following the turnings of the truck route. Near an overpass, a U.S. mail truck approached from behind. The driver must not have seen me; the inside corner of his overhanging van would have struck my left shoulder had I not moved quickly to the right. But then my front wheel bounced off the curb and I was headed back toward the truck. About to glance off its side, I gingerly pushed off with my left hand, righted myself, and fought to keep my balance until the truck was safely past. Good old Uncle Sam, to whom I pay many thousands of dollars in taxes each year, and in whose military forces I once served—well, not heroically, but I showed up—had nearly killed me. Talk about your "friendly fire."

Alternate 1 turned north and passed under the last of the Pulaski Skyway, where cars exited onto the reunited Route 1. Now the traffic was wall-to-wall. I decided to rest for a while.

In the middle of the street was a stone monument on a weed- and litter-filled island, so I crossed over there and hung out. The monument had a relief sculpture of someone by the name of George E. Blakeslee. "The Blakeslee Route" was written on the monument in large letters.

This wasn't just a rundown neighborhood in Jersey City; it was the Blakeslee Route! I was biking a trail hallowed by history—though one couldn't entirely ignore the "Fuck You" painted on the side of the monument in large black letters.

For something to occupy my mind while I rested, I tried to find out about Blakeslee and the monument.

"Never heard of Mr. Blakeslee," said an elderly black woman ambling by on the sidewalk, "but he must have been famous."

I crossed the street and talked to a gas station attendant. "What sculpture?" he said.

I pointed to it.

"Never noticed it before," he said.

A young, attractive woman approached on the sidewalk. She didn't respond to my question so I asked her again: "Excuse me, Miss," I said. "Do you know who George E. Blakeslee was?"

No answer. She was abreast of me now. She didn't look at me, just kept walking.

"Miss," I called in desperation.

No answer. Must have been something about not talking to strange men on bicycles.

After the trip I found an obituary for January 11, 1920, which said, assuming the reader would like to know, that George E. Blakeslee had been "one of the leaders in the good roads movement" in New Jersey and "a pioneer dealer in automobiles." I'm not sure whether George might have preferred to be dead and forgotten than remembered via such a sorry, disregarded monument.

After this brief cultural respite, I got back on the bike and headed north out of Jersey City along Tonnelle Avenue. The

Tonnelle Avenue section of Route 1 is known as Death Highway because of the spectacular accidents that take place there. I was hoping not to augment the road's reputation. Tonnelle was narrow, there was no divider or shoulder whatsoever, and the traffic had taken on an irritable quality. Occasionally, bits of sidewalk offered themselves, but I decided not to use them. They might soften me up, make me less attentive. It was safer to stay in the road and concentrate every second on survival.

Everything was dirtier now: the air, the buildings, the roadway—all grimy. I passed one dark cemetery after another. "Crematorium Entrance," a large sign announced. In the next cemetery an old man brushed bits of litter off a grave with a tiny hand broom. Nearby, a flock of pigeons pecked at a fresh grave.

A mile farther on, I came to a Chinese restaurant and decided to treat myself to a nice, late lunch. Chaining the bike, I strode out of the sunshine and into the dark, cool interior.

"How many?" the elegantly dressed Chinese headwaiter asked. I could hardly see him in the gloom. Somewhere an artifical fountain splashed.

"One," I said, following him through an obstacle course of empty tables, each set with blue and white crockery painted with Chinese scenes. I was the only customer in the place.

Why do headwaiters always ask how many when they can plainly see how many you are? Do they want to make you feel guilty for not markedly improving the establishment's financial prospects? Instead of being grateful that *someone* has arrived, they appear peeved that you aren't the advance scout for a large party of non-MSG-preoccupied big spenders, who will order many dishes each rather than sharing a few. Was it under the headwaiter's malign influence that I received, at the conclusion of the meal, a fortune cookie whose message to me, accompanied by a happy face, was, "Stay close to home in the coming days"?

Somewhat apprehensively, I got back on the bike. The sun was getting low, and I decided not to rest until I reached the George Washington Bridge.

I passed through Union City, then West New York, where I

caught a glimpse of the Empire State Building peeking over the rise. Just north of Ridgefield, Route 46 joined Route 1 for the trip to the George Washington Bridge, the same route I've taken countless times by car. The land rose steadily as the highway climbed the Palisades; I switched into a low gear.

The traffic was thickening, the drivers anticipating the bridge. I decided to be extra cautious. I hadn't come this far to get hurt at the last moment.

Up ahead the bridge loomed. Over my shoulder, the sun was almost gone, while, in front of me, the windows of Manhattan were bright orange. The bridge lights were already on. Cars were funneling into the tollbooths, and I was jammed in among them, with no defense but my little handlebar bell. The motorists didn't pay any attention to me as they jockeyed for position. I was just an obstacle, a nut on a bike.

A Lincoln Town Car started to pull out of its line to get into mine, which was shorter. The driver was turning directly into my body. He just didn't register that I was there on my bike in front of him. "Hey," I yelled. He finally stopped and, with a resentful look on his face, pulled in behind me.

I pedaled up to the tollbooth. The woman looked at me. "Hey Mildred," she called to an older woman in the next booth. "What about bikes?"

Mildred, obviously the veteran of the two, was making change. I couldn't tell whether she had heard or not. The driver behind me, the same gentleman who had nearly run me over and then given me a dirty look, leaned on his horn. Would Mildred please answer my toll collector? This place was getting less healthy by the moment.

"Let him through," Mildred finally yelled. "But make sure he doesn't go over the treadle; it'll mess up the count."

I passed through the toll area and quickly moved to the right and onto the bridge walkway. I began pedaling across the bridge, my eyes full of the great buildings of Manhattan, which stretched to the south along the Hudson River. Joggers steamed past me on the walkway. When I reached the midway point in the bridge and the New York state line, I rested for a while. Then I turned and pedaled back into New Jersey.

———————————

I won't go into how Patricia and my daughter Kate picked me up in the dark at the approach to the George Washington Bridge or how we got the bike onto the automobile rack amidst the traffic. Suffice it to say that it was the equivalent of fishing someone out of a river inches from a major waterfall and a complete urban adventure on its own. We considered ourselves lucky to be alive and didn't mind the four dollars in unnecessary tolls crossing and recrossing the bridge so as to be heading in the right direction into New Jersey.

What I do want to talk about is what happened after the trip was over and I was safely home. I felt real good about having biked eighty-five miles on Route 1 through New Jersey without a scratch; I felt indestructible and proud. But within a week back in the pastoral quiet of my hometown I was injured riding my bike. Two blocks from my house, a car shot out of a driveway. I saw it coming and tried to steer around it, but the bumper hit my right leg just above the ankle. I stood there on one leg, in shock, holding up my bike; I began to pass out.

Someone was screaming. I thought it must be me, but then realized it was coming from the car. The vehicle was halfway into the street, and the woman inside was pointing at me and screaming. Thinking she was in grave danger, I hobbled onto the sidewalk and approached the car. Leaning on it to keep from fainting, I asked her what the matter was. "I nearly killed you," she said accusingly. "I nearly killed you." Nothing like blaming the victim, I later thought. Regaining some composure she said, almost conspiratorially, "But don't worry; we've got insurance."

She didn't apologize and seemed relieved that I preferred to go to the hospital myself; I sure wasn't getting inside her car. Her parting words to me were, "My husband's going to kill me." Whatever misfortune had occurred seemed to have happened to her.

I staggered home, got my car out of the garage, and drove to the hospital. Luckily, the X rays showed no break, but my leg, up to and just beyond the knee, for a month put on a show of colors that rivaled the aurora borealis. And when it returned to normal, months passed before I had enough confidence even to bike around the corner. That fortune cookie in the Chinese restaurant had urged me to stay close to home in the ensuing days, and I had, and look what happened!

I've wondered since what kept me from getting hurt during the Route 1 trip. Perhaps it's because, on Route 1, I managed, as I had hoped at the beginning of the trip, "to insist on the integrity of the space I was occupying" and "to construct a corridor of calm through New Jersey." In short, I let Zen take over and, while I was vigilant, I was also trustful. I was neither too tight nor too loose, like a baseball player who *knows* he's going to bat well and proceeds to do so. On Route 1, I pedaled in a state of grace. It was almost a religious thing.

Of course, this could all be a lot of baloney. Maybe it was just luck that kept me from getting hurt on Route 1. Or maybe, because of the greater danger, I paid attention, concentrated on safety, on Route 1 in a way I don't when I'm near home; they say most vehicle accidents take place a few miles from one's home.

Or maybe it's just that Route 1 and I have a special thing about each other. Yeah, I think I'll leave it at that.

A Tale of Two Canals

My heart goes out to the old canal
A relic of days gone by
With its soggy banks
And rushes and danks
The haunt of the dragonfly

ANONYMOUS

There are landscapes that haunt. Not the majestic sugar maple outside my window as I write this, even with the fog swirling about its trunk. The maple is beautiful, but it lacks the hand of man, lacks history. It is the archaeological feeling of places where people have been and are no more that haunts.

Canals are just such haunting places. They are at that junction between man's works and nature, which is where one finds urban adventure and where I like to hang out.

Being basically a peninsula—and lying between the two great cities of New York and Philadelphia—New Jersey invited bisection by canals, and as early as 1676 William Penn was thinking of doing just that. By the 1830s two of these artificial waterways were in operation, and for a hundred years they were central to the state's commercial life.

Now they are slowly dissolving into the landscape; they lie just out of sight, abandoned, at the periphery of our lives. For years I lived in Morristown, around the corner from the Macculloch Hall Museum, without realizing that George Macculloch was the father of the Morris Canal, some of whose remnants may be found nearby. Earlier, I lived in Princeton, close to where the Delaware and Raritan Canal flows, yet I drove over it on a wooden bridge every day on the way to work without a glance.

One reason we tend not to recognize old canals is because they've deteriorated to the point where there isn't much to distinguish them from rivers. Walking along the Delaware and Raritan Canal, one observes its collapsing walls and thick vegetation, the cattails luxuriating in its shallows, the prodigious number of box turtles sunning themselves on its banks; and one thinks: What a quiet, lovely river! But then one comes upon some rusting lock machinery or a concrete mile marker, nearly engulfed by vines, and realizes that, while nature is fast taking over, evidence of man is still apparent. The ghosts of those who built and used this liquid highway are everywhere.

In the case of the Morris Canal the ghosts are less apparent, for the canal has been all but obliterated, from its origins at Phillipsburg to its terminus at Jersey City. In Newark, the city subway runs in what was once its bed, and elsewhere the canal is covered over by shopping malls and highways and condominium developments and Little League ballparks. But then, while standing at the outskirts of a West Jersey town, one may notice a kind of line heading across a vacant field which is entirely too regular or, while crossing that same field, stumble over some quarried stones or bits of shredded timbers—evidence that the Morris still haunts the area.

Finding the Morris takes detective work; it is difficult to follow it across the state from one ruin to the next—a bit like tracking a wounded animal. Discouraged, one fantasizes sending up a satellite with remote sensing capabilities and infrared film to map what is undetectable on the ground, as if searching for the local version of Peru's Nazca ruins. But then one is heartened by the sudden appearance of a curious-looking embankment or a shallow depression overgrown with weeds or an unnaturally tamed hill, formerly the site of one of the canal's inclined planes, where canal boats were hauled straight up a hill rather than floated through locks.

The spring after my bike expedition on Route 1, after conceiving a fascination for canals during a winter's armchair travel, I decided to experience New Jersey's canals for myself. With the ground softening at last and the first green shoots emerging, it was probably inevitable that earthy, sensual thoughts would occur to me more readily. That is perhaps why I was reminded, as I planned my expeditions, that New Jersey's form is often compared to that of a woman. The two canals cross her body—the 102-mile Morris at the high hills of her ample bosom, the 60-mile Delaware and Raritan at her cinched, narrow waist. Not unlike how the poet William Carlos Williams understood Paterson through the man he envisioned curled about the base of the Passaic Falls, I felt I might better decipher New Jersey's meaning by traversing these key points of her anatomy.

The Morris Canal

With the Morris Canal there is more to think about than to traverse. It is as if the genius of Americans is indicated twice in the Morris Canal—both in its frantic construction, which began in 1824, and in its systematic and comprehensive destruction in 1924. Certainly, it was inevitable the railroad would replace the canal, that what one could do in five hours would satisfy practical Americans better than what required five days. But the Morris was not just superseded; it was annihilated. It was dynamited, bulldozed, buried, as if it held some shameful secret all traces of which had to be expunged. In Europe one comes across old canals still in desultory use and two-thousand-year-old aqueducts far more intact than the nineteenth-century Morris Canal. That Americans would spend more dollars destroying the Morris than it took to build it suggests something less than attractive about our national character.

Nevertheless, one can launch an expedition along the route of the Morris Canal, discovering pieces of it here and there that escaped destruction or have been lovingly restored or are once again unemployed rivers. On May 13, 1989, the New Jersey Canal Society "traveled" the Morris, trucking canoes across New Jersey to the bits of canal that still retain water, including the best-preserved chunk of the canal at Waterloo Village, where the society has a museum. The society carried out a fantasy not unlike that of the chief character in John Cheever's story "The Swimmer," who traverses his native county via the swimming pools of neighbors and friends.

The society started its trek at the eastern terminus of the canal in Jersey City. They paddled about the Little Basin, where canal barges once were roped together for the trip across the Hudson River to Manhattan or were teamed with mules for the trip west. The travelers then stashed their canoes in trucks for the trip to the next canal site. It took all day, but the society, like toads migrating from one muddy puddle to another, managed to cross the state along the remaining waters of the Morris.

I have also followed the route of the Morris—in an automobile, I admit. I had no canoe with me, but I had a good time. In Jersey City I discovered that the Big Basin, just across the Hudson from Manhattan, is now the berthing place of the replica of Henry Hudson's ship, the *Half Moon*. In Clifton, behind a gas station, I came across a hundred yards of the canal. It has been converted into a minipark that overcompensates for the huge electric pylons straddling it by employing flowers and ducks and kitschy little paths. Just outside Paterson I found the shadow of the canal where it once traveled along the base of Garrett Mountain just off present Interstate 80. And in Boonton I walked up the steep hill of Plane Street, now macadam but once covered by the rails of one of the Morris's inclined planes.

Farther west I discovered a tiny, waterless piece of the canal in a farmer's field—or, rather, it discovered me, for I nearly fell into it. Coming through the thick stubble of the previous summer's cornstalks, I found myself perched on the lip of what looked like the foundation of a long-abandoned house. The stone walls were held together by vines, which I grasped as I descended into the canal. I jumped down the last five feet, a mistake. The canal bed was overgrown with raspberry brambles, and I got badly scratched. When it was time to leave, I had difficulty climbing out of the canal—indeed, I momentarily panicked, thinking I might be trapped down there forever.

Undeterred from further adventure, I traveled to Port Warren. It's just a place, not a town, where Jim Lee lives atop a hundred-foot hill, surrounded by rusting remnants of the machinery that once hauled boats up what was then Inclined Plane 9 West. Cables lie in the grass, rails in the bushes. Looking out at the countryside below, I thought of *Fitzcaraldo,* German director Werner Herzog's magical 1982 film in which a mad Irishman decides to build an opera house at Manaus on the Amazon. The only way he can get building materials to Manaus is by hiring hundreds of natives to drag his large iron vessel out of a jungle river, over a mountain, and down into the navigable tributary beyond. On Inclined Plane 9 West one has heroic feelings not unlike those which a love of opera evokes.

Jim Lee has been restoring his piece of the canal for years now. It started as his hobby and became his life. The Morris inspires this kind of devotion. As Jim has written in his book, *The Morris Canal: A Photographic History,* "I think that the Morris Canal was a beauty spot on the map of New Jersey, a place where men could work and boys and girls could play; a place where a Sunday walk on the towpath was sheer contentment; a place where there were more fish than fishermen."

More than the Delaware and Raritan, which still flows between the two rivers that provide its name, the Morris Canal arouses nostalgia in canal lovers, perhaps because there is so little of it—a sense of loss being key to nostalgia.

The great majority of New Jerseyans, nevertheless, are utterly unaware of the Morris. Sleepy Port Morris is one of several high and dry towns or hamlets in northwestern New Jersey which, with no major river or the ocean in sight, have *port* as part of their names—such places as Port Murray, Port Colden, Rockport. Each was once a center of canal activity, but today the only vestige of the canal one usually finds in such places is the creek on the edge of town, long since returned to its proper banks after one hundred years of lending its waters. I asked a high school student why his town is called Port Morris.

"Dunno," he said, looking at me blankly.

"Did it have anything to do with the Morris Canal?" I persisted.

"Dunno," he said.

If history didn't excite this young man, it was unlikely engineering would either. The Morris was a stupendous mechanical achievement. In addition to twenty-three lift locks, there were twenty-three inclined planes on the Morris, each a poem to American ingenuity. The canal traveled upward from Jersey City 914 feet until it reached its high point at Lake Hopatcong, its main source of water, and then started down toward Phillipsburg. It rose and descended 1,674 feet crossing the state, 16.5 feet of vertical movement per mile.

By comparison, New York's famed Erie Canal makes but 1 foot of vertical movement per mile, and the Panama Canal rises and falls only 85 feet during its fifty-mile voyage between oceans. Boatmen on the Morris were a species of mountain sailors. Indeed, the Macculloch Hall Museum called a 1991 exhibit on the Morris "New Jersey's Mountain-Climbing Waterway."

The Morris was celebrated around the world. The British writer Frances Trollope, who in her *Domestic Manners of the Americans* had few nice things to say about Americans, showed uncharacteristic enthusiasm for the Morris Canal when she visited it in 1831:

> We spent a delightful day in New Jersey, in visiting, with a most agreeable party, the inclined planes . . . on the Morris Canal.
>
> This . . . most interesting work . . . at one point runs along the side of a mountain at thirty feet above the tops of the highest buildings in the town of Paterson, below; at another, it crosses the falls of the Passaic in a stone aqueduct sixty feet above the water.

Frances Trollope's enthusiasm for the Morris's inclined planes is echoed by anyone who has ever taken an interest in canals. The Morris utilized Scotch turbines, which functioned like giant rotating lawn sprinklers when the canal's waters poured into them from a height. The power of the turbines was transferred to a drum and cable that hauled eighty-ton coal and ore barges on rails up and over the high hills of New Jersey, doing the work of five or six locks. The power of water! A little water can motivate a waterwheel to turn great stones and grind corn; not much more water can haul heavy boats up mountains.

Morris Canal boats spent so much time on the rails of inclined planes they were almost amphibious—like World War II assault vehicles that, after crossing the waves, rode up over the land. Approaching an inclined plane, a canal boat typically was floated onto a cradle with a wheeled undercarriage and winched up or down the railway. It then entered the next water section of the canal on a new level. With a total distance in inclined planes of over five miles, the Morris ran quite a little railroad of its own.

Sometimes a trip on an inclined plane was less than smooth. The heavily loaded boat *Electa* was making its maiden trip on the canal in the early 1830s. Just as it started down the inclined plane at Boonton the chain to which the cradle was affixed snapped. A newspaper told the story:

> Gathering momentum, the boat and its tons of pig iron went hurtling down the plane with the captain's wife and two children aboard. It hit the water just as a toboggan might and splashed water for hundreds of feet.
>
> Not only that, but its momentum was so great it skittered along the surface like a modern hydroplane, then lifted its bow at a crazy angle and finally hurdled over an embankment twenty feet high and landed with a crash in some trees.
>
> White-faced and trembling bystanders rushed to rescue the captain's wife and family. As the wife emerged uninjured from the cabin they breathlessly explained just how the breaking of the chain had caused the accident.
>
> "Why," she said, "it was a mighty fast trip, I'll

allow, but I thought that was the way the thing worked."

Not long after exploring the Morris, my little knowledge of inclined planes came in handy. I had come home with an interesting boulder for the garden in the deep well of my automobile trunk. Never mind how the boulder got into the trunk; that's another story. The problem now was how to get it out. I had no block and tackle, and the boulder weighed five hundred pounds easy.

While I was standing in my driveway, pondering what to do, Phil Herbert drove by. Phil always likes challenges, but now there were only two of us trying to pull five hundred pounds of dead weight out of my trunk—and at great peril to our backs. Remembering the Morris, I got some thick boards, angled one up in my trunk and another down from my bumper. I told Phil about the Morris Canal's inclined planes, and he said, "Egyptian slaves dragged rocks up pyramids like that."

"Yeah," I said. "That's how I know how to do this; I'm descended from those slaves."

We inched the boulder up one side of our little inclined plane and down the other to the ground. Well, actually, we inched it up, but we had only started inching it down when it came roaring down by itself. We leaped out of the way and it fell in my driveway with a sickening thunk, much like the *Electa* when it charged down the Boonton inclined plane. Phil and I managed to drag the boulder in among my roses a few feet away, where it sits to this day and has no immediate plans of going elsewhere. If the reader ever visits I'll show it to you, and if I'm not home, it's the big brown one near the yellow climber.

The Morris Canal, through the sheer audacity of its engineering, reminds one that the people who design rides in Disneyland are not called engineers but "imagineers." The Morris Canal must also have been built by imagineers. Better still, by Rube Goldberg. It was made up of as many parts—inclined planes, locks, water sources, pieces of canal—as any Rube Goldberg contraption. Only it worked.

The Morris Canal also reminds one of the Toonerville trolley from the old "Toonerville Folks" comic strip. Like the Toonerville trolley, the Morris headed through the most unlikely of terrains, over hill and dale, mission and destination seemingly known only to itself.

Also like the Toonerville trolley, the Morris Canal fascinates us because its technology is on a scale large enough and simple enough to understand, a welcome relief from the unfathomable mysteries of computers. Recently, when the PC on which I am writing this had to be repaired, I watched breathlessly as a technician opened it. I was about to know, firsthand, the meaning of life.

Nothing was inside the computer but a fan, some chips lined up in rows, and a bit of circuitry. The meaning of life, if my computer held the answer, remained as much a mystery as ever.

In contrast, the Morris offers the surety, in the words of the old spiritual, that the "hipbone [*is*] connected to the thighbone." The Morris is a cast-iron thing in an increasingly miniaturized, automatized, lightweight, plastic world. And while the canal is virtually gone, its sparse remains evoke a reassuring solidity, suggesting that oft-repeated phrase: "They don't make 'em like they used to."

The Delaware and Raritan Canal

Just before Frances Trollope visited the Morris Canal, she crossed the waist of New Jersey from Trenton to New Brunswick and all but wished that the Delaware and Raritan Canal, then being dug, was ready for use. Ascending the Delaware River from Philadelphia, she was forced in Trenton to leave "our smoothly-gliding comfortable boat for the most detestable stage-coach that ever Christian built to dislocate the joints of his fellow man." After this journey, she was surprised to find herself "still alive and on board the boat which was to convey us down the Rariton [*sic*] River to New York City."

The Delaware and Raritan still follows the route of Frances Trollope's stagecoach ride. At a point seventy feet above sea level, it extracts water from the Delaware and sends it flowing toward New Brunswick, where, at close to sea level, it enters the Raritan. Once this water carried so much Pennsylvania coal to New York's furnaces that the D & R was the number-one canal in America in total tonnage carried. The cargo it transported across New Jersey in two days formerly took two weeks to make its way down the Delaware, around Cape May, and up to New York City via an often perilous ocean route. Today the D & R transports no cargo but its own waters across New Jersey; it has a sleepy, pastoral look. Yet the canal is more valuable than ever for the drinking water and pleasure it provides.

The D & R has been transformed into a sixty-mile-long by hundred-foot-wide linear park through the very heart of the eastern megalopolis. Just beyond the canal's leafy bower is a sixth-grade geography text of highways, towns, factories, and shopping malls, but being so long and so meagerly policed, the D & R is that rare park where you can feel truly isolated and free. You can fish, stop to cook a meal, pee *en plein air,* pick wildflowers, take your clothes off, camp out for the night. Since the only access to the canal is at rare highway intersections, you can traverse the waterway for miles without seeing another person, and when, surprisingly, someone does appear far down the towpath, it is usually a solitary jogger or a poet or a pair of lovers seeking that special solitude that only the canal offers.

If one's experience today of the Morris Canal is archaeological, that of the Delaware and Raritan remains fluvial; if the Morris inspires contemplation, the D & R inspires adventure. I thought of canoeing the length of the canal and still hope to do it someday. I also thought of walking it, but I had only a weekend, so biking the sixty-mile towpath seemed the best way to go.

I knew my Raleigh Gran Prix would be too high-strung, too temperamental for a trip like this; the bumpy towpath would destroy its thin wheels and tires, especially since it would be carrying lots of extra weight—a pup tent, a sleeping bag, food. Phil Herbert keeps a mountain bike stashed in his garage, and he agreed to lend it to me. I tried to leave him my Gran Prix as collateral, but he refused, saying, "Just get this mountain bike back to me in one piece. I don't want your Raleigh piece of shit."

I didn't like Phil insulting my Raleigh, which had so nicely transported me on my Route 1 trip, but I didn't say anything; I needed that mountain bike. Besides, Phil didn't mean any harm. Grousing is just his style.

Anyway, his mountain bike was great. It had wide, nubby tires and a thick frame—a mule of a bike, like the mules that once walked the same path, towing fifty-ton coal barges across New Jersey. Today, no mule could tow anything on the D & R because of the large trees that have grown up between the towpath and the water since commerce ended on the canal. Nor could heavy draught boats move along the silted canal. But beauty has replaced utility as the canal has taken on the patina of age. The scale of everything along the waterway is small, almost European; the only sound one hears in its vicinity is the gurgle of slow-moving water.

I began my D & R trip at Bull's Island, where a weir dam, like the one in the Raritan that Phil Herbert and I rocketed over on our canoe trip to New York, raises the level of the Delaware so water will enter the canal feeder. In summer, the island is covered with campers' tents, but now it was a muddy, solitary place, gloomy except for the meager efforts of the wan, early spring sun to brighten things up. The island's mass grave of Irish immigrant canal laborers, who died in the cholera epidemic of 1832, contributed to the gloom.

I sat on the little bridge over the feeder that connects Bull's Island to the shore and looked down at the dark water. It was a pure meditation thinking of the sixty-mile trip that awaited each drop. And awaited me as well.

I got on the towpath and began pedaling the narrow strip of land between the canal and the Delaware River. The feeder flows southeast some twenty-two miles, paralleling the Delaware all the way to Trenton. There the canal proper begins with a 150-degree turn and heads northeast for thirty-eight miles to New Brunswick. The present, complete canal is shaped like a V, with the point of the V at Trenton. Unlike the Morris, which insisted, whatever the obstacles, on heading straight across New Jersey, the D & R, more sensibly, was dug in the valleys of whatever rivers were at hand—the Delaware, Stony Brook, the Millstone, the Raritan. The D & R worked with nature; the Morris overcame it.

Perhaps that is why the D & R has survived and the Morris has not. Of course, hunks of the D & R have been lopped off. Once it was shaped like a Y instead of a V, a six-mile segment from Trenton to Bordentown meeting a fate not unlike that of the entire Morris. And the last three miles of the canal in New Brunswick were obliterated a few years ago by that city's Route 18 freeway.

But if it bears the scars of civilization, most of the D & R still placidly wends its way across the state. Occasionally its towpath gives out—washed away by a storm or covered over by debris—but it is passable for most of the canal's sixty miles, and it is the perfect sylvan companion for a bike ride, as are the charming little towns along its route.

I came to Stockton, the town with the small hotel that inspired the song which begins, "There's a small hotel / with a wishing well / I wish that we were there / together." The circa 1710 hotel was just up the street from the canal, so I pedaled to it and found someone to give me a cup of tea and sat in the garden and looked at the famous wishing well.

Back on the towpath, I pedaled down to Lambertville, once a major canal port. When the canal closed to commercial traffic, Lambertville went into a steep decline; but recently it has come back as a chic town, the canal feeder now wending its way between antique stores, art galleries, restaurants, and bed-and-breakfasts.

I passed this terrific seafood restaurant I'd often heard of, The Fish Tale, and pedaled up to its door and made a tentative reservation. Then I called home from the restaurant pay phone. Patricia said "great" to our driving down to Lambertville for dinner the next Saturday night and said she'd start looking for a babysitter.

Then she asked if, while I was in Lambertville, I would check out Beard's, an antique store she'd read about in *Antiques &*

Fine Arts magazine. "They're supposed to have a terrific Stickley and Arts and Crafts movement collection," she said.

Patricia is seriously into antiques. So much so that I am often forced to walk around our house with a tube of Duco cement in one back pocket of my jeans, a screwdriver in the other, gluing and tightening furniture that, unattended, would soon disintegrate. Don't get me wrong: I like old things too. But more than once I've fantasized feeding those antiques one by one into the fireplace and replacing them with furniture you can actually sit and jump on. Our children, Kate and Joshua, feel the same way.

Dutifully, I pedaled down Bridge Street and found Beard's and was delighted that it was closed—not only because this would slow the migration of antiques to our house and ensure no further erosion of our economic position but also because I was short of time. I was determined to camp out on the trail, and there were many miles and all of Trenton to get through before this day was over. Trenton, whatever my urban adventure ideals, was not where I fancied spending the night in a pup tent.

The city was, nevertheless, fascinating terrain to cross on a bike. Walled off from it by a chain link fence, with occasional signs affixed saying "City of Trenton, No Trespassing," the canal passes through backyards and behind state government buildings, alongside city streets and under tiny bridges. Once children skated on the canal only to discover, too late, that although the canal moves slowly, its ice is often fragile. The chain link fence saves lives, but it is the barrier against which all of Trenton's blowing litter comes to rest. A veritable library of old newspapers is plastered along its entire length.

Sometimes as I crossed the city I found myself locked in by the canal fence; other times the fence barred me from the canal, and I had to parallel it as best I could on side streets and through vacant lots. I pedaled along more than one burned-out ghetto street and past bars and beauty parlors and bodegas, the uniformly black and Hispanic residents eyeing this strange, middle-aged gringo on a mountain bike with more than a little curiosity.

Wending my way across town, I reached Old Rose Street. Here, at the confluence of a litter-filled lot, an abandoned railroad trestle, and the Route 1 freeway, the waters of the canal pour into a broad culvert and are swallowed up by the city, flowing for 1.2 miles under Route 1. What to do? Hoisting my bike over the fifteen-foot wall of the freeway was impossible. I would have to parallel Route 1 through the wilderness of swamps, chemical plants, boiler factories, and ancient dumps that make up this part of Trenton until I somehow found the canal again.

I must have pedaled four miles to make the one mile to the place where the canal reemerges, and all the while I was anxious, not knowing if I was on the right track. Finally, I came down a potholed industrial street, where yellow trucks were lined up to enter a parking yard. I asked a security guard if he knew of a canal thereabouts.

He looked at me and at my bike, not saying anything. Then he said reluctantly, motioning over his shoulder, "There's a little creek just beyond that tire dump. But it ain't no canal."

I decided to take a look anyway and pedaled into the dump, where high hills and veritable Matterhorns of tires occupied the land like some alien life-form. I skirted the edge of the tire mountains, afraid that even the tiniest vibrations from my bike might set off a rubber avalanche. On the other side of the tires was a "creek," but it was a creek with a towpath. I was back on the trail.

Good thing, too, because the day was fast ending. I pedaled rapidly down the towpath, passing through the last of Trenton's suburbs and into Lawrence Township. A few miles farther on were the remains of Port Mercer, now a tiny community of just a few white houses. This is where I intended to bed down for the night. Erecting my pup tent in the middle of the towpath, I chained my bike to a tree. Then I walked to the diner in the nearby Mercer Mall and ordered mashed potatoes and roast beef and chocolate cake for dinner. I had earned it.

It occurred to me after giving my order that I had barely spoken to anyone all day; that's how secluded the canal is. I rather liked my sudden self-sufficiency and vowed to be less gregarious from then on. But I haven't kept the promise. Maybe urban explorers aren't meant to be laconic.

Back in the pup tent I listened to the hoofbeats of phantom mules coming along the towpath until I finally fell asleep and dreamed of water.

———————

I awoke when the first birds began talking in the trees above me. After returning to the twenty-four-hour diner for a hot breakfast, I packed up and headed down the towpath. The canal had taken on a bucolic aspect. Daylilies were everywhere emerging on the bank; the fresh canes of wild roses rioted through the underbrush.

In Princeton the canal is carried in an aqueduct over the Millstone River. It isn't an elevated aqueduct like the one on the Morris that once spanned the Passaic River, giving the impression to onlookers of boats sailing down the sky. The D & R at Princeton is just encased in iron and concrete, allowing the Millstone to flow under it.

Afterward, the river, which Phil and I had employed on our canoe trip to New York, parallels the straightflowing canal, sometimes coming so close as to almost touch, other times frivolously wandering off over the meadows. When the river flows alongside the canal it is difficult to tell one from the other—except after heavy rains, when the canal, whose level is kept constant, appears unchanged while the Millstone is for some days a raging torrent that spreads out over the landscape.

I passed the remains of a lock in Kingston. The lock tender's home is still in place, including a small shack out back where tolls were once collected and telegraph messages received. Now it serves as a tiny canoe rental office. Beyond Kingston, most of the concrete canal mileposts still stand, ruined obelisks some three feet tall, located at the side of the towpath. They have two sets of engraved numerals, the miles back to Bordentown and the miles ahead to New Brunswick. These markers were as much comfort to me as they must once have been to mule skinners eager to know how far they had traveled and how much farther they had to go.

At the next town, Rocky Hill, I explored the remains of the

Atlantic Terra Cotta Company on the left bank. All that remained were some crumbling stone walls, but, in 1913, thousands of tons of decorative terra-cotta were shipped from this spot down the canal to New Brunswick and from there to New York City, where they were used to sheathe the Woolworth Building, then the world's tallest structure, and do to this day.

Refreshed by this cultural interlude, I pedaled past one lovely canal village after another—Griggstown, Blackwell's Mills, East Millstone. These towns bustled with activity when the canal was in its prime, but now they were still, almost museumlike. White, early nineteenth-century houses lined the canal bank, and in their precincts people were following quiet pursuits—fishing, gardening, reading the Sunday *New York Times* on wisteria-garlanded porches.

I bought some peanuts and figs for lunch in Chester & Sons, the general store just off the towpath in East Millstone, and sat on the canal bank to eat them before mounting up and pedaling on. Soon the Raritan River swept in from the west, and the Millstone River merged with it. The canal, however, made an acute right turn and now paralleled the Raritan. It is not until New Brunswick that the Raritan is tidal and capable of floating anything larger than a canoe.

I was now pedaling a narrow strip of land, with the wide Raritan off my left shoulder and the canal off my right. The strip was created from the dirt and rocks thrown up as the canal was dug and separates the canal from the Raritan as much as it provides a foundation for the towpath.

I had reached the industrial suburbs of New Brunswick, where the canal took on a ruined aspect. There was debris on the banks and shopping carts in the water. Sumacs and other weed trees grew out of the rock walls of the far bank, and the towpath was often obstructed and once blocked entirely by a minidump of asphalt roof shingles. I steered around it gingerly but, even so, almost fell into the Raritan.

Near the New Brunswick city limits, alongside Landing Lane bridge, the canal poured unceremoniously into the Raritan. The waters that had begun their voyage across New Jersey at the

Bull's Island feeder, and which I had observed there, had prematurely reached their destination. What had formerly been the canal's last three miles was now the Route 18 freeway.

This wasn't, however, quite the end of my trip. I had heard that on the other side of New Brunswick, near my office, is the ruin of the long outlet lock, and I wanted to see it. Cutting through the city, I pedaled along New Brunswick's main drag, George Street, and then down to the Raritan again, where, alongside the Rutgers University boat house, I found the remains of the lock.

The outlet lock's timbers were still largely intact, and its flat stone walls still in place, but its massive doors were gone and it was full of garbage, its only water that which seeped in with the tides of the Raritan. The isolated lock was once a busy place where incoming and outgoing canal traffic were separated. Now it was a lock without a canal.

———

I had experienced both canals, one largely by contemplating its meaning, the other by biking its length. The experiences, while different, had been equal in their intensity. There may be another way to close these musings on New Jersey's two canals, but I don't know of one more fitting—albeit overly sentimental to some tastes, including my own—than the second verse of the anonymous poem, written shortly after the closing of the Delaware and Raritan Canal to navigation in 1932, that introduced this essay. It speaks for itself:

> My heart goes out to the old canal
> And so it goes out to all
> Of the time-gilded store
> Of things of yore
> That have drifted beyond recall.

Afoot on the Double Deuce

Oh highway . . . you express me better than
I can express myself.

WALT WHITMAN,
"SONG OF THE OPEN ROAD"

Having twice biked large portions of New Jersey, walking it seemed a natural for my next adventure, which took place the summer after my canal excursions. For a while, I toyed with traversing the length of the state, north to south, but the width was challenge enough. My notion was to experience the state in cross section—hiking from rural to exurban to suburban to urban New Jersey, about twenty miles and one day of each, moving west to east as urban adventure usually requires in my part of America. The best way to make that kind of expedition, I decided, was along Route 22. It would get me nine-tenths of the way across the state; from there I would see.

Route 22, like Route 1, is pure New Jersey—that is, a little of this, a little of that. Beginning at the Pennsylvania border and continuing straight across the state almost to its eastern limits, 22 runs through farms, towns, suburbs, and cities. The western section of the highway is quiet and easygoing, but much of the eastern is a thirty-mile-long shopping center. There the frantic traffic spawns such Route 22 nicknames as Blood Alley, the Psychiatrist's Delight, and Catch 22. Route 22 appears regularly on the National Highway Safety Council's list of ten worst highways. Still, New Jerseyans have a certain affection for it. They call it the Double Deuce.

"Come on feet, don't fail me now." That's what I was singing under my breath. My right foot was hurting awfully as I ascended, under the weight of my backpack, the steep hill from the Delaware River and entered the town of Phillipsburg, which perches on its banks.

I was beginning to think my neighbor, Ralph Thompson, the insurance man, was right. Ralph had dropped me off in Easton, Pennsylvania, just across the Delaware from Phillipsburg; he had an appointment farther west in Pennsylvania. Before leaving me he had said, "Better be careful. People get hit walking on highway shoulders all the time. We've got statistics on that at the office." If I was already in pain, only fifteen minutes into the hike, the chances of my emerging unscathed after seventy-nine more miles seemed less than promising.

The pain in my foot was different from the tendinitis that had bothered me on my Manhattan walk. This time the boot was rubbing my skin raw, and I knew if I didn't do something quick the trip might be over before it started.

Luckily, I soon came to a drugstore—the old-fashioned kind, with a floor of black and white hexagonal tiles and a brightly lit soda fountain. Off in a dark corner was the foot products stand. I'd always wondered who patronized these products; now I knew. There were items for treating corns, athlete's foot, calluses, sore heels, blisters, bunions, hammertoes, and other ailments too disgusting to name—all mounted on dusty, yellow Dr. Scholl's cards.

The druggist recommended something called Moleskin. "We sell a lot of Moleskin," he said, as if to suggest that Moleskin was the latest fashion; if you valued your position in society, you would get some immediately. I bought two packages, even though Moleskin sounded more like a skin affliction than a product designed to ameliorate one.

As I sat outside on the curb, gingerly wrapping my foot in the Moleskin, two little girls in dirty dresses watched me intently. "Whadya doing?" they wanted to know. These girls, who seemed straight out of a Walker Evans photograph, were emblematic of Phillipsburg, which, with its hills and slanting row houses, looks like a 1930s coal-mining town. Unlike so much of New Jersey, which is sucked into the vortexes of New York or Philadelphia, Phillipsburg's back is to the megalopolis and life is peaceful, if dull. In Phillipsburg, everyone's idea of a big time is to walk across the Delaware River bridge and go shopping in Easton.

My foot problem assuaged by the Moleskin, I walked to the outskirts of town and got on Route 22, which here was a quiet country road, nothing but farmers' fields and high hills and wild-flowers as far as I could see. If ever there was a place that didn't fit New Jersey's stereotype, this was it.

Suddenly, however, I knew myself to be very much in New Jersey, where weather forecasting may be at its most inexact anywhere on the planet. Although nothing but blue skies had been promised for that sparkling spring day, it now began to pour. Reaching back, I pulled the Totes from my backpack. I felt silly hiking the shoulder of the highway with an umbrella, but other cover was unavailable and I had nowhere to go, nothing to do, except head up the road. I slogged along, enveloped in that wet world, peering out at occasional ghostly automobiles.

I reached the tunnel of a highway overpass and huddled there on the sloping concrete sidewall. It was a lonely, dark world under there, notwithstanding the legend "Booley Loves Sally" painted high above on a girder. How had the heroic Booley gotten up there, and did he still love Sally? What if this sign, in which one was tempted to place so much romantic stock, was now, for Booley and Sally, like an unwanted tattoo acquired at a rash moment?

At both ends of the overpass rain poured down in sheets, almost obscuring the landscape beyond. Pigeons fluttered in and out of their nests in the steel understructure, my only company except for the pitiless eyes of passing motorists, who probably thought I was a vagabond, a homeless person, which, for the present, I was.

The rain finally stopped—just in time, because I couldn't have taken another depressing moment in that concrete underworld. As I passed out into the open and on down the road, the sun came out and the earth steamed. It seemed the right time to follow up on an old idea.

In the Introduction I mention how I often craved stopping my car and heading up the nearest hill just on a whim. My notion now was to leave the highway and travel cross-country, straight across the land, oblivious not only to fences and farmers' fields but to railroad tracks and roads. I wanted to experience the terrain as the Native Americans had, unhindered by the obstacles now placed in the landscape. We say "as the crow flies." Don't we have the same rights as crows?

There was a high, eroded ridge beside the highway. I climbed it and the hill beyond and entered the woods. But it was no good up there. I was forever tangling myself in brambles and tripping over fallen trees. Looking at my compass when I should have been watching where I placed my feet, I nearly went off a small cliff disguised by brush. The only trails were meandering deer paths in the woods and cow paths in the open fields, and, apparently, these animals had never shared my desire to head east by some expeditious means.

I was getting nowhere. I hated giving up, but there was nothing to do but fight my way back to the ridge above 22 and skid down onto the highway shoulder again. So much for crows! Plainly visible was the spot where I had left the road a full hour before, only two hundred yards back toward Phillipsburg.

Resigned to walking the highway now, I discovered the attractions of the shoulder, where every pebble, every blade of grass, is an event. On the shoulder a continual struggle goes on between asphalt and grass. First grass forces itself up through cracks. Then workers come along and poison it with herbicides or cook it with fresh tar. A few months later the grass is back.

A lot went on on the shoulder of Route 22. Countless dead animals—opossums, raccoons, groundhogs, deer—rotted beside the road or were being tanned into leather on the highway. You know there's a dead deer ahead well before reaching it, and the sickly sweet smell stays with you long afterward; it's on your clothes, on your skin, in your mouth. New Jersey, the most densely populated and toxic state, has the greatest deer population per square mile. Go figure.

In addition to natural history, there is human history by the roadside, man's spoor. In the space of an hour I came across enough artifacts of our civilization to set up a museum. Glass fragments from an automobile accident (recent or ancient? it was impossible to say) sparkled on the asphalt like tiny ice cubes. There was a Sears bill, a dime, a set of keys, a quarter, a marble, a red checker, and somebody's IRS 1040 tax form, all filled out and ready to go.

Also on the roadside was a once-elegant man's hat—the bright feather still in place—a woman's shoe, half a transistor radio, an unopened pack of Camels, and, peeking out from between two dandelion clumps, a torn, damp centerfold from the previous December's *Playboy* magazine—Suzy Nelson of Des Moines, Iowa, still desirable with her pouting lips and full breasts. Hobby: stamp collecting; favorite book: *The Catcher in the Rye.* Ah, Suzy, what a catcher you were! Had you ever imagined ending up on a New Jersey roadside, pumping up the blood of a lonely urban adventurer who ordinarily insists skin mags are dreary and beneath his dignity?

These roadside discoveries entertained me as I walked along Route 22. By late afternoon, I had reached the state Correctional Institution for Women outside Clinton. Its fence came almost to the highway's edge, and I rested there, mindful that this was the very fence America's most famous fugitive, Joanne Chesimard, escaped over some years before after having been convicted in the murder of a state policeman on the Jersey Turnpike.

The prison fence seemed as good a place as any to take stock of my own situation, which was grim: my body ached, it was starting to rain again, and night was coming on. I had planned to sleep by the side of the road in my pup tent, but now I thought: Nuts to that; I want a bed and a bath! I knew of a motel, but it was six miles farther down the road. Six minutes in a car, but two and a half hours for me.

It was dark when I finally limped into the Fountain Motel in Lebanon, no doubt named for the cracked and toppling fountain out front that looked as if a truck had backed over it. The room clerk told me about a diner half a mile east of the motel, but I couldn't have survived another half-mile trek, much less the other

half mile getting back to the motel. Walking across New Jersey
once was all I'd signed on for. I went to my room, stripped the
now frayed Moleskin from my foot, took the hottest bath ever
survived by a human, and had a bag of M & Ms and a can of
sardines from my pack for dinner. Then I fell into bed.

————

I awoke encased in cement; that's how my body felt. I tried
sitting up, but it hurt too much. The way I finally got out of bed
was by sliding onto the floor. Now I was lying on the floor. My
nose was pressed between the tall, dirty fibers of the shag carpet,
and in a moment my eyes started to itch, allergies kicking in. I
had to get up off that carpet fast. Struggling to my hands and
knees, I grasped the bedsheets and pulled myself to my feet.

Stiff and aching though I was, there was a great sense of
freedom just walking out of the motel and onto the highway. No
checking the oil, no fussing with the baggage in the trunk. Nothing to concern myself with except moving my two feet down the
highway toward that diner.

"Where'd you come from?" asked the motherly waitress in the
Spinning Wheel Diner as I removed my pack and eased my body
into a booth. When I told her I was walking across the state, she
stopped taking my order and stared at me.

I ordered two complete breakfasts, a Number 1 and a Number
3, and headed for the men's room—a luxury never to be passed
up on a hike. When I returned, the waitress said, "That men's
room is in another town." I smiled agreeably, thinking this must
be one of the jokes of the place. It turned out the Spinning Wheel
sits astride two towns; my booth was in Lebanon, the men's
room in Whitehouse. Check it out in case you're ever there. This
information may not overly entertain the reader, but it enlivened
some otherwise solitary moments for me.

After breakfast I got back on Route 22, crossing the highway
so as to face the oncoming westbound traffic. Now that I was
farther east there was more traffic, and the shoulder lane all too
often was transformed into an exit I had to dash across. With
each passing mile, more roadside businesses appeared, mostly of

the semirural variety: plant nurseries, equipment rental stores, recreation vehicle dealers. The woods had thinned out, and poison ivy now luxuriated by the side of the road, its tendrils reaching for my ankles. Most people fear poison ivy in the woods, but that isn't where it grows; it grows where the landscape has been disturbed: on roadsides, in backyards, along fences. Like sumac and crabgrass, it is a plant that likes being around people.

Other signs of approaching civilization: there were fewer dead animals on the road, and these were mostly of the domestic variety, dogs and cats; and a lone jogger, appearing out of the morning mist like an apparition, passed me on the shoulder, breathing heavily and sweating, not meeting my eyes.

In the afternoon the sun came out hot. I craved a frothy milk shake and stopped at every roadside stand, but to no avail. The only milk shakes offered were the same premixed sludge I've always disdained at McDonald's. I'd have settled for fresh orange juice, but I couldn't get any of that either. America must be an underdeveloped country if such simple pleasures are virtually unavailable.

It was late afternoon when I reached the outskirts of Somerville. Here, at the dividing line between West and East Jersey, the country abruptly ends. Route 22 takes on its characteristic form: wall-to-wall malls, fast-food restaurants, used car lots, gas stations, motels, supermarkets, diners, discount furniture stores, drive-in banks, and go-go bars.

I had dinner in a Howard Johnson's and then, as darkness approached, sat outside on a bench deliberating where to spend the night. The air was crisp, the sky clear. If I was ever to sleep out on the trip, this was the night. But where, in a parking lot? Then I noticed that the grass median between the east and westbound lanes of 22 was wide here, maybe a hundred feet across. And there was a copse of trees fifty yards up the highway. Maybe I could set up my pup tent in there. Even with cars going by on both sides of the highway, no one would notice me.

I called home from the Howard Johnson's. I was only thirty miles away and thought one of my kids might like to come down and camp out with Dad. Patricia was willing to drive, but the kids didn't want to come. Kate was having her own kind of sleep-over—five girls were expected at our house momentarily. And Joshua's two favorite television programs, *The Simpsons* and *Married with Children,* were having specials that evening. What did it mean that he preferred to watch programs about dysfunctional families than to camp out with his father?

Feeling lonely and disheartened, I waited for near dark before pitching my tent and crawling in for the night. Then I worried. I worried that I would be murdered in the night. Then I worried that the police would roust me out of there and throw me in jail for violating some obscure law. Then I *really* worried that a tractor trailer would go out of control, crash through the thin trees surrounding me, and squash me flat in my sleeping bag. Each time the light changed up the road I sweated, listening to the traffic accelerating by. I kept flashing to an image of my sleeping bag converted to a body bag.

My only consolation was that at least neither of the kids was here with me in all this danger. Maybe I wasn't such a bad father after all. When I was all but reconciled to staying up all night, the noise of the traffic grew fuzzy and I finally fell asleep.

In the morning I emerged from my hideout, crossed the eastbound lanes, and had breakfast in a Dunkin' Donuts. I was stiff from sleeping on the ground and from two days of steady hiking, but I was hurting less than I had the day before, so my body was toughening up, getting used to this. And my spirits were high: I had survived a night in the middle of Route 22!

The rest of that day I walked through the crazy quilt of towns that line Route 22, flowing seamlessly into one another: Bound Brook, Green Brook, Plainfield, Scotch Plains, Mountainside, Westfield, Springfield, Union. Actually, it wasn't the towns I was walking through but their commercial districts, which in each case had been shunted out onto Route 22. On the highway, it was impossible to discern which town you were in—unless you already knew that Two Guys was in Plainfield, Rickel's in Watchung.

Walking through these towns presented a new challenge. There was no shoulder and no sidewalk, so I hiked the parking lots of the commercial establishments that line the road—progressing from the parking lot of a bowling alley to the parking lot of a Burger King to the parking lot of a pizza parlor to the parking lot of a Toyota dealer. I felt as if I had invented a new cross-country sport. If we keep paving the world, there may be Olympic competitions someday. What? Okay, forget it.

I had to be especially careful on the strip of highway that runs for four miles between Springfield and Union. There cars dart on and off the highway to both right and left because the center median, where I had slept the night before, is no longer grass and trees; it's back-to-back rows of stores. With stores also bordering the margins of the east and westbound lanes, this makes four parallel rows of commerce. Even Las Vegas, the most famous strip in the world, can't boast that.

"You can buy anything on Route 22," people say in North Jersey. And this most intense of commercial strips isn't at the approach to a big city or on its way to anywhere in particular; it's just out on the highway, a veritable thicket of pop architecture and signs. The neon giant of Channel Lumber towers several stories over the highway. The *faux* paint cans on Siperstein's roof are the size of oil storage tanks. And the stores in the strip sport these terrific names. There's Teenage Bedrooms and Foam World and Leaning Tower of Pizza and Simply Socks and Hamburger Oasis and Condom City and Foodorama. I wonder why *rama* has been appended to the names of so many American stores in recent years. I'm sure it has nothing to do with the Hindu god Rama. I make a point of never setting foot in stores whose names end in *rama.*

Peeking over the horizon in Union is what looks like a battleship. It's huge and gray and has decks, railings, portholes, a superstructure, and even a metal sailor aloft, flashing signals. Inside, there are heavy ropes and lifeboats hanging everywhere; the men's room has "Buoys" on the door. The Flagship once claimed to be the biggest hot dog stand in the world; then it was a nightclub where Frank Sinatra sang. Now it's a giant furniture store.

Whatever Route 22 may be for shoppers, it's no paradise for pedestrians. There is only one pedestrian bridge in ten miles of strip, and you can't cross at the red lights because there aren't any. The lights were removed to keep traffic speeding along and to limit rear end collisions. Also, to get to stores on the other side of the highway, motorists use the U-turns that cut through the store-filled median every half mile, frantically exiting from the high-speed lane on one side of the highway and entering the high-speed lane on the other side, where a truly original merge must be accomplished. It's dangerous enough for cars, so no wonder one rarely sees people outside of automobiles on the Route 22 strip.

I did meet two Swedish hitchhikers on the strip. They had caught a ride at the entrance to the Lincoln Tunnel in Manhattan but had been stalled for several hours now without a ride. Even if someone wanted to pick them up, no one could, because there was no shoulder to pull onto. I asked them where they were trying to go. "Vest," they said, looking at me plaintively. "Ve vant to get ooout of here."

I had what may be the ultimate pedestrian experience shortly after meeting the poor Swedes. Walking among shopping baskets in front of a Pathmark supermarket, I spotted what looked like a juice bar on the other side of the highway and was determined to get there. For two days I had been craving a glass of fresh-squeezed orange juice. This is what I did to get it: cross the Pathmark parking lot, dash across the two lanes of speeding traffic on the westbound side of the highway, cross the north parking lot in the median strip, get through the back-to-back stores (to save time, I went in and out the front and back doors of Leather Luxury and Pinky's Pizza), get through the south parking lot in the median, race across the two lanes of deadly traffic on the eastbound side of 22, and, finally, get across the parking lot in front of the juice bar. I earned that glass of orange juice.

There are places where it's even tougher getting across 22 on foot because there is no median, only a high concrete divider known as the Jersey Barrier. The barrier eliminates head-on collisions, but pedestrians have to scale it somehow. I watched in horror as a middle-aged woman in sneakers, carrying a shopping bag, stood on the narrow top of the barrier in Mountainside, the wind from passing cars buffeting her body. She had successfully crossed the eastbound lanes and now was balancing on the barrier, waiting for a break in the westbound traffic. She must have been a veteran, however, for, as soon as the traffic cleared, she hopped down and scurried across the westbound lanes of traffic. I wish I could have talked with her. Perhaps she was a colleague, another urban adventurer.

The Route 22 barrier is dangerous not only to pedestrians; when there's a hard rain it holds back water and the highway floods. There is a tiny brook between Kitchens by Dolly Madison and Arthur Treacher's Fish & Chips where I briefly stopped to rest and cool my feet. It was a peaceful spot, strewn with boulders and covered with wildflowers. But in August 1973 seven inches of rain fell in four hours on the Watchung Hills above the highway. A dam burst, and a massive wall of water charged down this very creek bed and onto the highway, where the barrier kept it from escaping. When the water retreated, five commuters were found drowned in their automobiles right on Route 22.

Thinking of this story gave me a chill—or was it that the sky had clouded over and evening was coming on? I got moving again, fast. In Union, I passed under the Garden State Parkway. I was once again pleasantly surprised by the perfect quiet under such a major highway, but when I emerged on the other side it began to rain. Luckily, a quarter mile farther on, I came to the Garden State Motor Lodge and decided to check in. Camping around here was too much of a challenge even for me.

But was this a motel or a penitentiary? The clerk was behind bulletproof glass, and she talked through a microphone and took my money with a retractable tray. I received a piece of plastic the size of a credit card that said "ADT Security Systems" and was informed that this was my key. "It also turns on the television," she said matter-of-factly.

I inserted the card in the door of room 243, and it sprang open. Then I put the card into a slot in the television set. On one channel Dan Rather was describing the Mount Pinatubo volcanic eruption in the Philippines. On another, three men, two women, and a dog were making love.

———————

It was pouring when I woke up. The news said acid rain, fallout from Mount Pinatubo, was descending on the metropolitan area. I checked the other channel. Men, women, and dog were still at it. Who says there is no continuity in American life?

It was rush hour, and the traffic on Route 22 was a frenzy of wet rubber and steel. The highway had narrowed, and now there were almost never any shoulders or parking lots to shelter me from the traffic. My umbrella kept turning inside out in the gale. Then, as if I wasn't feeling bad enough, some guys in a moving van roared by and yelled "Asshole!"

Soon after, I concluded they might be right. I had entered the long curving tunnel under the railroad in Hillside, where there was only a curb six inches wide to walk on. In the darkness, I inched sideways, my chest flat against the grimy stone wall of the tunnel, my arms outstretched. Trucks sped by, throwing up sheets of water. Was this the dreaded acid rain, and would it eat through my clothes? I crept through the tunnel, a human spider, feeling that this time I had put myself too much at risk. This wasn't adventure; it was suicide. Twenty agonizing minutes passed before I finally emerged—filthy, scared, and feeling more than a little stupid—from the tunnel.

Two miles farther on, Route 22 abruptly ended in a maze of cloverleafs near Newark Airport. I wasn't sure which direction to turn to reach the eastern edge of the state; and mile-long mistakes on foot are not tolerable the way they are in automobiles. Climbing over a steel and concrete barrier, I slogged through a low area of cattails and climbed over a chain link fence onto a highway. It was my old friend, Route 1. If I wasn't mistaken, I could walk Route 1 briefly northward and then enter Jersey City.

It was delightful to be back on Route 1 and on the same shoulder that had temporarily afforded me the luxury of safety during my bicycle trip on that highway. To make things even better the rain stopped, and I began to dry out. Of course, the air was sulfurous, and I was surrounded by a landscape of chemical factories and junkyards. The few weeds by the side of the road looked like mutations, and the only "wildlife" I encountered was a huge, dead dog lying atop a pile of oily plastic sheeting that must have fallen off a truck. Still, Route 1 proved to be my Cumberland Gap through the industrial hub of the state—from Newark over the foul Meadowlands and into Jersey City, where I left Route 1 and took to the city streets.

Being in a city after three and a half days on the highway was a novelty, and I ambled slowly, enjoying the simple pleasure of sidewalks. There were so many people, so much to look at. Everything in poor, dull Jersey City seemed to sparkle. Journal Square's mélange of architectural styles and signs somehow recalled a European plaza, and the Irish, Italian, and black neighborhoods I passed through seemed not rundown but exotic. It felt as if, after a lot of hard work, I was on a much deserved vacation.

As I passed through the city, the land dropped off, and I could sense the Hudson River below. As I rounded the corner of a warehouse, the Holland Tunnel, which courses under the Hudson to Manhattan, came into view. Cars were lined up, red and green lights flashed, bells rang as tolls were collected. I approached a tollbooth and asked if I could walk to the midpoint of the tunnel on the catwalk. That would really be the state line, and I fancied reaching it as I had on my Route 1 trip, when I biked to the center of the George Washington Bridge. But they wouldn't let me into the Holland Tunnel on foot.

Still, I had walked across six counties—Warren, Hunterdon, Somerset, Union, Essex, and Hudson—and I felt as if the state and I had special claims on each other, as if I belonged to it and it to me in a way other citizens could not appreciate. I had also proven to my satisfaction the simple fact that, large as the earth may be, you can walk almost anywhere if you want to badly enough.

Sea Monsters
of New Jersey

It amounted to something being a raftsman on
such a raft as that.

MARK TWAIN, *HUCKLEBERRY FINN*

On the high banks above the Delaware River the early morning
fog was not too thick, but by water's edge, where I was standing,
it was pure soup. All I could make out were the gaudy colors of
the seventy-six iron rafts stretched out along the beach and the
outlines of the nearest men and occasional women, perched on
their rafts like tank crews awaiting the grim signal for war. Everyone was silent, serious.

At 8:29 the one-minute warning sounded. A hush fell over the
thousands of spectators on the hillsides; my left eye twitched.
Then the cannon went off, and the captains of each raft, in a Le
Mans start, charged across the open field and down the slope.
We saw Kern Strickland trip and do a complete somersault, but
he must have landed on his feet because in an instant he was
racing toward us along the beach. We pushed off into the water
and he jumped aboard just as the current swept us out into the
river.

Thus began the most grueling four hours and twenty-four minutes of my life. Strapped onto what looked like a medieval tor-
ture device, our crew sat in individual cockpits, Kern and Jerry
Lystad in front, Phil Donadio and myself in back, connected to a
single chain-drive mechanism that pushed the paddle wheel. With
the resistance of the water it was like nonstop pedaling uphill on

a bicycle in tenth gear. If you tried to rest, your legs would get mangled in the machinery, which never stopped rotating.

The Delaware River Raft Race courses between the New Jersey and Pennsylvania banks for twenty-four miles—not quite a marathon, but long enough. It begins at Smithfield Beach, five miles north of the Delaware Water Gap, and ends below Belvidere, New Jersey. Along the way are stretches of white water, including a mile of class VI rapids at a place ominously named Foul Rift.

The origins of the race are obscured in legend. As the story goes, Ebeneezer Scroggins, proprietor of a tavern along the Delaware, was surprised one day in 1734 by a band of Iroquois. Rolling a keg of beer into the river, Scroggins mounted it, attempting to escape with the current. Undaunted, the Indians pursued him astride their own kegs. At Foul Rift the agitation of the water and heat of the sun combined to explode the beer kegs, and in the confusion Scroggins escaped.

Positively no one believes this story, but it provides cultural compost for the Delaware River Raft Race, in its ninth year when I was a competitor. Two elements from the Scroggins legend are central to the race: enough beer is consumed on raft race weekend to float a sizable navy; and the rafts must be constructed of kegs—actually fifty-five-gallon steel drums.

The race has an elaborate set of rules. Each raft must have from three to six crew members, and there are two classes of rafts, A and B. A class A raft has a single hull of barrels, while a class B has a double. Class A rafts resemble racing shells and are usually faster. B rafts are heavier and wider, more like what you imagine when you think of a raft. The raft I was on was a B. There were fifty-two B rafts in this year's race, twenty-four As. Trophies would be awarded to the first three rafts in each class to finish the race.

All rafts must have at least four "undistorted barrels"—that is, barrels that have not been modified in any way. Streamlining is allowed at either end of rafts, and crews go to elaborate lengths to achieve this. Some crews cut up old canoes and weld bows and sterns at both ends of the line of barrels; others, more intent on fantasy than speed, apply fake smokestacks or convert the ends of their rafts into funky metal sea monsters. Coming down the highway on its trailer chassis, such a raft looks like a cross between a racing car and something out of Dr. Seuss.

The rules call for rafts to have "propulsion and maneuvering systems," but they must be "devices which do not utilize energy stored prior to the race start." One year, a raft had a solar panel, but it put out only enough electricity to power an eggbeater. Most rafts use oars, paddle wheels, sails, or some Rube Goldberg combination. Some crews mount bicycle frames on their barrels with drive mechanisms attached to multiple paddle wheels. Our raft, the *Snuffle-upagus,* named for the Sesame Street character, had a thirty-foot mast and sails in addition to its paddle wheel.

These rafts seem more the product of an urban and industrial imagination than a rural one. They evoke thoughts of primitive submarines or of early ironclads—the *Merrimac* and the *Monitor.* They look like they don't belong out on the water but in the Smithsonian Institution—suspended from cables like the Wright brothers' airplane or the *Spirit of St. Louis.*

The day after each year's race, crews are already at their drawing boards, designing next year's raft. Some try to get a little more speed out of a competitive raft. Others scrap inefficient rafts altogether and start from scratch. Over the long winter, in snow-covered New Jersey garages, basements, and auto body shops, the world's most fantastic rafts take shape.

Late in the winter after my Route 22 hike across the state, I was admitted to the Lebanon, New Jersey, basement of Ernie French, captain of the three-man *Top Banana* raft, which had taken first place in class A several times. I had heard of Ernie and wanted to see his iron raft for a magazine story I was thinking of writing about the Delaware River Raft Race. Little did I know that I would soon find myself in the race as a participant.

Secrecy was the watchword in Ernie's basement. It looked so much like a defense plant that I felt uneasy without a plastic ID clipped to my shirt. There was an elaborate machine shop down there that included a drill press, a couple of lathes, an oxyacetylene welder, a Lincoln arc welder, and a Dewalt radial saw.

Ernie's burly crew leaves nothing to chance. Each spring they fly over the Delaware in a Piper Cub to check for changes in the river such as new sandbars. They get advice from Princeton University's rowing coach. They've even gone so far as to leave around a spurious design of their raft at the traditional captains' meeting a month before the race to confuse competitors about their plans. The payoff was evident: several huge trophies on a built-in bookcase in Ernie's basement, all earned by *Top Banana.*

This year the *Top Banana* crew was trying to produce the lightest, strongest raft possible. Their original raft weighed eight hundred pounds ("a real ice breaker," Ernie said), but they hoped to get this year's raft down as close to two hundred pounds as possible. They were adding a rearview mirror and using light-gauge barrels. Said Ernie, who earns his living at the Ford motor plant in Edison: "Engineering's the name of the game."

If so, I was lucky to have been asked to join the crew of the *Snuffle-upagus,* all of whose members are engineers. Kern Strickland and Phil Donadio are mechanical engineers who work at Picatinny Arsenal in Dover, New Jersey. Jerry Lystad is an electrical engineer at AT&T Long Lines in Bedminster. It was through Ernie French that I got on the *Snuffle-upagus* crew. He had heard that their fourth crew member, also an engineer, had a bad back and that *Snuffle-upagus* was looking, as Ernie put it, "for another pair of legs."

We worked on *Snuffle-upagus* weekends in Phil Donadio's backyard in Long Valley, New Jersey, where he tinkers with an old house trailer and five different automobiles in his spare time, including a 1964 Alfa Romeo he's been restoring for years. In their late thirties, Phil, Kern, and Jerry still fantasized about being race car drivers. As a substitute, they poured their energies into the raft race.

I was the amateur of the group. All I could do to improve the raft was paint. I felt better when we needed a twenty-four-tooth fourth-gear sprocket and I found one on a ten-speed bicycle Ralph Thompson, my next-door neighbor, had put outside his house during spring cleanup week. Except for a little rust the bike looked perfectly good to me, so I checked with Ralph to make sure he really meant to throw it out. He did. After removing the fourth-gear sprocket, I put the bike in my attic and have been cannibalizing it for parts to fix family bikes ever since.

Earlier versions of *Snuffle-upagus* had been in the raft race three times but had never won. This year the crew had high hopes. There was a new paddle wheel with articulating blades that always remained perpendicular to the surface of the water. And the mast and sail was an addition. If the wind blew from the north, we could greatly improve on the previous year's speed.

As raft race weekend approached, I decided to get myself into shape. Every day I ran five miles and did one hundred push-ups and one hundred sit-ups. I was feeling terrific until we took the raft out for a trial run on Lake Musconectcong two weeks before the race. We discovered two defects: one of the barrels had a tiny hole, and soon the raft began to list to one side; and my legs totally cramped up after just minutes of pedaling. We took *Snuffle-upagus* back to Phil's house, where he welded the defective barrel. I added an hour on a bicycle machine and leg lifts to my daily workout.

By Saturday morning of race weekend, June 10 and 11, *Snuffle-upagus* and I were ready. Our crew left Long Valley in a caravan, Phil pulling *Snuffle-upagus* on a trailer up front, me proudly bringing up the rear. At the Smithfield Beach parking lot we entered a long line of rafts and their crews, ready for the weigh-in. One by one, rafts were inspected to make sure they conformed to the rules. Then pictures of each raft and its crew were taken, and all crew members had to sign waivers absolving race organizers of responsiblity in case of injury or death. Paperwork taken care of, we took our raft down to the beach to get it ready for the next day's race.

After bedding down *Snuffle-upagus* for the night, we drove up a dirt road to a nearby large field set aside for participant and spectator camping. No one would be allowed on the beach overnight except race officials, who would guard the rafts against sabotage. In past years, rival crews had set rafts adrift in the river or punched holes in their barrels or painted insulting graffiti all over them.

The campsite was a nautical Woodstock. Half-naked children ran about, and tie-dyed shirts, candles, and balloons were being hawked. Hundreds of tents were squeezed into a space so small everyone got to know each other pretty quick. When night fell, a women's rock band played and there was dancing, copious quantities of beer, the musky smell of marijuana joints being passed around, and a whole pig roasting on a spit. Fireworks were going off all around the field.

You could tell who took the race seriously—mostly the class A crews, who camped on the edges of the field. I spotted Ernie French and his teammates way off on their own and strolled over there. They stared at me—not in the mood for idle chatter—though perhaps they were even less talkative because I was now with *Snuffle-upagus,* an adversary and a potential spy. Ernie and his boys were eating spaghetti with grim determination, loading up on carbohydrates. For many crews the race tomorrow was just a hoot; for *Top Banana,* it was the Olympics.

The *Snuffle-upagus* crew was somewhere between the extremes. We cooked steaks and drank a lot of beer that night, but, at Kern's insistence, we bedded down early.

At five A.M. Sunday morning I was awakened by the partyers in the big army tent next door who apparently had never gone to sleep. As the sun came up they were still jumping about—crowing now like roosters, trying to wake the whole camp. I peered outside, but the fog was so thick I couldn't even see the offending tent. An object flew through the air and clanged off one of its aluminum poles, and someone yelled, "Shaddup." But all he got for his trouble was a big "Haw haw haw."

The guys in the army tent were the *Blazing Barrels* crew. Later that day we encountered them on the water, drifting along, more than one of them fast asleep. As we sailed by, one of the conscious raftsmen almost toppled into the water as he mournfully lifted his can of Budweiser in salute.

At 6:30 I crawled out of my pup tent and joined Kern, Phil, and Jerry for a breakfast of hot oatmeal, bananas, and orange juice. I wanted a cup of coffee bad, but Kern said, "No coffee. Once the race starts, there's no way to pee."

Down at Smithfield Beach there was an immense amount of activity in the fog. It was more like the Indianapolis 500 down there than *Huckleberry Finn*. Bullhorns blared instructions to all crews, someone was pounding out a dent in a barrel, National Park Service speedboats coughed just offshore, last-minute mechanical adjustments were being made, and everyone was getting into bright orange life jackets. I thought the bulky jacket would impede my movements, but Jerry said I should wear it: "Your legs will be so tired one hour into the race you'll drown if you fall overboard." He gave me some gray heating-duct tape to wrap around my ankles to keep them from getting smacked by the rods of the pedals as they came around. We loaded our provisions—a barrel of Kentucky Fried Chicken and a case of Gatorade—and tensely awaited the start of the race.

When the race began and Kern leaped aboard, we pedaled like crazy to get clear of the beach. The paddle wheel creaked and slowly began to turn and grip water. Then, as we moved out into the Delaware, the sun broke through, streaking the landscape with shafts of light.

We got an excellent start because our paddle wheel was in the center of the raft. Most paddle wheel rafts had them hanging over one side and banged into each other trying to get off the beach. And oar raft crews had to pole themselves out to open water before they could row, while we quickly slipped through into the clear. Earlier I had considered myself lucky just to be in the race. Now, as we approached the first island, I wanted to win.

Ten minutes later my hopes were dashed. The wind was blowing from the south, right in our faces, so the sail would be less than useless. And when we approached a power line, we had to lower our aluminum mast, eating up precious time and energy. The class A rafts began to pass us. *Top Banana* was in the lead, but almost even with it was a raft called the *Long Orange*, which seemed to be matching Ernie's crew stroke for stroke. Soon most of the sleek class A rafts were ahead of us, and we had to content ourselves with what was happening in class B.

By forty minutes into the race, two class B rafts were already past us, the blue, oar-powered *Mother Ducker,* which had taken second place in class B the previous year, and a bicycle raft, *Sneaky Pete.* Close behind us was another bicycle raft, mysteriously named *#151,* its crew of five men and a green-eyed woman with marvelously sculpted legs gazing down at us impassively from their high seats. Just before the Delaware Water Gap we began to catch *Mother Ducker.*

At the Gap, the rafts were spread out over the Delaware's surface in a fluvial carnival the likes of which would have inspired Handel to compose a second *Water Music.* Thousands of spectators were on the walkways of the Interstate 80 bridge and along the banks of the Gap, shouting and honking their automobile horns. They would follow us downriver to various vantage points, as would rescue boats, ambulances, and a helicopter. Many of the spectators wore T-shirts with the names of their favorite raft and had hung banners off the bridge urging them on. "Go Blazing Barrels," one banner read. The slushing noise of our paddle wheel blurred most sound, but a portion of the shouting did seem to be directed toward us. Just before passing under the bridge I spotted Patricia with Kate and Joshua waving frantically to me, but my delighted acknowledgment was so late I didn't know if they saw it.

Just below the bridge we pulled past *Mother Ducker.* I was excited. If we could pass one of last year's class B champions. . . . But *#151* was still on our tail. "Come on, guys," Kern yelled, and we put even more effort into moving our leaden legs. My legs hurt so much I thought my bones would crack. But *#151* was only fifty feet behind us, traveling in our wake, with five crew members on bicycles at a time, the other nonchalantly standing on the deck resting. Every few minutes a crew member jumped off a bike and a fresh and rested one jumped on its seat and hit the pedals running. How I envied their rest periods. I fantasized being invited to join their crew and beginning my tour of duty with a nice long rest.

Emerging from the Gap, with eighteen miles still to go, *#151* passed us so easily it was scary. The bastards had been playing with us, getting us to wear ourselves out before they finished us off.

But we were still in third place, still eligible for a class B trophy. Okay, I told myself, we'll take third. Not bad. Not bad at all.

Soon, however, the red, white, and blue oar raft, *Spirits of Belvidere,* came out of nowhere and passed us effortlessly. Okay, fourth. No trophy, but respectable. But then, below the Columbia-Portland bridge, *Mr. Clean,* another bicycle raft, passed us. It didn't seem fair.

Now a paddle wheel raft, *Riffraft,* slowly crept up on us. This was too much. It seemed essential not to let a raft like our own pass us.

Our legs were past feeling anything, but we summoned the strength to keep *Riffraft* just behind us for five miles. The whole race was transformed into a contest between *Riffraft* and us. In my exhaustion, I thought: If we stay ahead of *Riffraft* I can die happy. But if they pass us, then the whole race, the whole weekend, my whole life is ruined.

My knees ached, and my nemesis from the Manhattan hike was reappearing: tendinitis, along the back of both ankles. I tried massaging my knees and ankles while I pumped. Lord, if only we could stop for a minute! At the Belvidere bridge *Riffraft* caught us. I felt depressed and beaten. Sixth! But Kern shouted, "Look at the bright side: there's forty-eight class B rafts behind us."

That made me feel a little better. Okay, sixth. There were no class B rafts in sight behind us, so maybe we had a lock on sixth. I relaxed and tried to enjoy the scenery. A class A pedal raft pulled alongside and slowly passed us, one of its crew members conspicuously reading *Gentlemen's Quarterly* while he pedaled. "Yuppie scum," Jerry Lystad muttered.

We could now hear the roar of Foul Rift. As we entered the white-water maelstrom, bobbing about almost out of control, I noticed we were gaining on *Riffraft.* It was lower in the water, did not move as quickly through the rapids as we did. Kern saw what was happening too. "Let's take her," he yelled. Further energy was summoned out of our hopeless legs.

The crew of *Riffraft* turned to see us and were alarmed at our approach. They steered for the right side of the river, where the water ran more swiftly.

And then the unbelievable happened. With a scream of tormented steel, *Riffraft* went up on some rocks amidst the raging water. The *Riffraft* crew got out of their vessel and clambered about trying to pry the raft free. But they were stuck good. Only a trifle guiltily, we exulted as we swept by.

Riffraft was still stuck on the rocks when we went around the next bend in the river. Later we learned that by the time the raft finally got off the rocks its paddle wheel was twisted and one of its barrels punctured.

Ahead was the finish line, an abandoned railroad trestle. It was covered with people, as was the landing beach just beyond. As we swept under the trestle, thousands of people cheered for us. I felt enormously proud. We had taken fifth in class B, and twentieth overall, which meant that we had beaten even some class A rafts.

We pulled in just off the beach to await our turn at the National Guard crane that was lifting rafts out of the water. I swung my legs out of the cockpit, but when I lowered them into the water they didn't work; there was no feeling in them whatsoever. I clung to the raft, afraid of being swept away. Two race officials saw that I was in distress and waded out to me. Grasping each other's wrists, they lifted me in an arm sling and carried me ashore. I stood there, unable to move, holding on to a tree.

Patricia and the children came gliding toward me through the trees. Kate and Joshua put their arms around my waist, and I was able to let go of the tree and lean on them. It was delicious being dependent on my two young children. I think they enjoyed the role switch fully as much as I. We stood there for what seemed a long time, Patricia beaming at the scene, all of us savoring the moment. Even though feeling was returning to my legs, I was in no hurry to break the spell.

Then a commotion broke out farther up the bank. I could see some pushing and shoving under the trees, but by the time I hobbled up to where the brawl had been taking place it was over. I learned that the fight started when the *Long Orange* team received the trophy for first place in class A. *Top Banana* argued that *Long Orange* should be disqualified because of the fraudulent construction of its raft. One crew member took a swing at another, and the remaining members of both crews jumped into the fray.

I found Ernie French wandering around, looking disconsolate, a bruise on his chin. "Look at that thing," Ernie said, pointing to the *Long Orange* raft. "The whole bottom is smooth."

A week after the race, at the request of Ernie and four other class A captains who sided with him, race officials took apart the *Long Orange* to inspect it. They discovered that its unnatural smoothness was due to its crew having fabricated their own barrels; they were the exact dimensions of fifty-five-gallon drums, but they had no lips; when fastened together, they made one unbroken surface. It had always been assumed all raft drums would be industrial ones bought secondhand; but the rules said nothing about homemade drums. Technically, *Long Orange* could not be disqualified, and they were allowed to keep their first-place trophy. "We'll write more specific rules for next year," the chairman of the race committee said. "That would be nice," Ernie French said angrily.

I called up Kern Strickland to discuss these developments and asked what his plans were for *Snuffle-upagus* next year. Kern said they were going to retire her.

"Retire her?" I asked, incredulous.

"Yes," he said. "We want to build an A raft next year. I've got this new idea on powering it. Besides the paddle wheel, we'll have a screw, just like a motorboat. We'll pump the screw with our arms and pedal the wheel with our legs. It'll take some coordination, but we'll have almost twice the power. We might even beat *Top Banana* and *Long Orange*." Then he added, almost in a whisper: "But don't breathe a word about this to anyone."

8

Blood Ditch

I never beheld a scene so utterly desolate.

FRANCES TROLLOPE, *DOMESTIC MANNERS
OF THE AMERICANS*

Frances Trollope was talking about the mouth of the Mississippi,
but there are scenes just as desolate in New Jersey, places where
the customary wall-to-wall towns and malls have given way to
wilderness. Burlington County is a good example. The mysterious and virtually unpopulated Pine Barrens occupy much of the
county, and a large portion of the rest is swamps or blueberry
and cranberry farms. Burlington, like much of South Jersey, is
nothing like the industrial nightmare out-of-state visitors see along
the northern reaches of the New Jersey Turnpike. Truckers on
their CB radios often refer to New Jersey as "the Garbage State,"
but, in Burlington, you get the feeling New Jersey might actually
be the Garden State after all.

Burlington is New Jersey's largest county by far, as big as
Bergen, Essex, Passaic, and Union counties put together, with
plenty left over for the giant Fort Dix and McGuire Air Force
Base complexes. It is also the only county that extends across the
entire width of New Jersey, from the Delaware River to the
waters of the Atlantic Ocean. That appealed to my imagination. I
wondered if I might cross Burlington's seventy-five miles under
my own power, "from sea to shining sea" so to speak.

I planned my trip for January largely because that's when I
had a long weekend free. Winter didn't worry me because I find
it easier to keep warm when it's cold than cool when it's hot. I
also rather liked the off-season aspect of the trip. There's nothing

quite like an adventure or a vacation when nobody else is taking one.

After studying innumerable maps, charts, and pamphlets, I figured I could bike across most of Burlington County in two days. But the maps showed the Atlantic end of the county as inaccessible marshland, with no roads, no inhabitants, no nothing—more like Louisiana bayou than the ordinarily built-up New Jersey shore. There was no way to bike into those far extremes of Burlington County. There was no way even to hike in there.

I called Phil Herbert for advice. "Sea kayaks," he said. "We can get in there with sea kayaks."

We? For once, Phil seemed to have dropped the pretense of his reluctance. It turned out he had a sea kayak in his garage along with all his other gear; he'd never used it and was dying to try it out. He thought a buddy at the firehouse had a sea kayak I could use.

I'd never even heard of sea kayaks, and I didn't like the idea of breaking up my adventure by switching from bike to boat. Not to mention that while I wasn't worried about being cold on my bike, putting out to sea in January seemed slightly nuts. But what choice did I have if I wanted to reach the end of the county?

I knew it was a rationalization, but I felt better about the mixed aspect of the trip when I imagined it as a three-day biathlon. I would pedal up, jump off the bike, and, without pausing, push off in the sea kayak. This wasn't just an adventure; it was a sport. With that fantasy fixed in my mind, I arranged a rendezvous with Phil for the third day of the trip near the Atlantic Coast.

I began the trip in Burlington City Friday morning, in a park alongside the Delaware River. Patricia was trying a case in court in South Jersey and dropped me and the Raleigh Gran Prix off on her way. I had on long underwear, jeans, gloves, a skiing cap, and this wonderful French windbreaker with space-age insulation, but the wind was blowing fiercely off the water.

"You sure you want to do this?" she said.

"Sure."

"Well, stay warm," she said, leaving me alone by the waterside in a cloud of exhaust.

In the park, sea gulls wheeled and landed. Just downriver was the bridge to Pennsylvania and just upriver Burlington Island, the site of the first European settlement in New Jersey in 1624. But it was cold, so I didn't tarry by the river but pedaled the ten-speed up High Street into town.

Burlington City still has an old-time feeling, heightened by the diagonal parking on High Street and the tracks on Broad Street on which freight trains occasionally lumber through the center of town. I pedaled along the brick sidewalk, stopping to have a look at 457 High Street, the row house where James Fenimore Cooper was born. Next door, at 459, James Lawrence, naval hero of the War of 1812, once made his home. He was the guy who said, "Don't give up the ship." I thought Lawrence's motto might just prove inspiring during the water part of my trip.

Carefully crossing Route 130, the major truck highway that roars through the middle of Burlington, I headed east on bucolic Route 541. As the roadside strip gave way to a welcome bit of open country, I experienced a key difference between cars and bikes. Seeing the countryside from behind an automobile windshield is like watching television; you're part of the audience. On a bike, you're a key actor in the show.

And I would always rather do than watch. Talk to anyone about anything rather than watch Oprah or Donahue. Have sex rather than watch it, read about it, or talk about it. Play touch football in the backyard with friends, wives, and kids rather than watch the Super Bowl. The only real Super Bowl is one you play in yourself. No wonder sports fans go berserk at athletic events, even when their team wins. They've been watching others for hours, bottling up their adrenaline, and they finally explode in frustration. They want to be part of the show.

Mount Holly is only six miles from Burlington City, and soon I was coasting down the flanks of the 185-foot hill, originally covered with holly, which gives the town its name. Burlington County is so flat, this was one of the few times on the whole trip I used anything but fifth gear.

Before High Street bottomed out at Rancocas Creek I reached the 1796 Georgian-style Burlington County Courthouse, the oldest continually used county courthouse in the United States, or so the plaque outside claimed. I stopped and ate my backpack lunch—a tuna sandwich, an apple, and a bag of Doritos—on a sunny bench in front of the courthouse, musing happily on how biking offers the best pace at which to experience history, not too fast, not too slow, with the extra joy of never having to worry about parking or empty fuel tanks.

Leaving Mount Holly, I turned east on Route 38. This highway had a shoulder—which was a relief, for traffic now moved by me at great speed and I felt vulnerable on the bike. I tried to conjure up some of the Zen karma that had protected me on my Route 1 bike trip, but the wind from the trucks threatened to blow me over and the bits of broken glass, abandoned mufflers, and flattened animals were a constant menace. There were enough dead possums and raccoons on the shoulder for an enterprising person to go into the fur business.

It was now three in the afternoon, and I needed to make tracks; there were only two hours of daylight remaining and I wasn't sure I'd get the whole two hours, because a weird brown fog was rolling out of the woods and low places. Turning south on Route 206, I kept the pedals on my bicycle spinning as fast as my legs would tolerate, paying scant attention to the wintry dairy farms passing in the gloom.

The moment I pedaled across the northern limits of the Pine Barrens, which occupy fully one-fourth of New Jersey, the trees became dwarfed and the soil beside the highway gave way to sand. It was as if someone had drawn a line across the land.

The Pine Barrens were once under the sea and will be again, no doubt, when the polar ice caps melt and the ocean rises. But my problems were more immediate: it was getting dark, and I hadn't seen a motel since Mount Holly. I knew that up ahead, at a place on the map called Red Lion, Route 70 crossed Route 206. If there was no lodging at that intersection I was in trouble.

Luck was with me: there was a Red Lion Motel whose neon sign advertised "In Room Movie, Waterbeds, Special Day Time

Rate, Room Phone, Cable T.V., H.B.O." I would have no occasion to enjoy these amenities, but the motel was still a bargain at twenty-eight bucks. And the proprietor just shrugged when I mentioned parking my bike in my room. South Jersey is a lot more relaxed than North, I thought, remembering how I had been grilled about the bike at the motel on my Route 1 trip.

Ray's Cabaret, just down the road, had a sign flashing "Family Dining," but everyone inside was at the bar. The regulars turned as one person to look at me. Still, things seemed wholesome enough: An ancient Bee Gees song was playing on the jukebox and spaghetti was offered—"All You Can Eat."

While waiting for my meal, I tried to find out about the name Red Lion. Partly I wanted to know, but partly I just wanted to make conversation. I was lonely; I hadn't spoken to a soul since Patricia had dropped me off in Burlington that morning. One fellow, wearing a John Deere cap, told me Red Lion was once a stagecoach stop. Another, in overalls, told me there was a Red Lion airport nearby. "But why *Red Lion?*" I asked. They both shrugged.

———————

When I awoke Saturday morning in the motel, my legs wouldn't work properly, wouldn't stretch to their full length. Hobbling along, several inches shorter than my normal height, I walked the bike down Route 206, hoping I would limber up.

At the Route 70 crossroads circle I came upon the Red Lion State Police barracks. There was a stone lion outside painted red, but none of the officers inside had a clue to the mystery of Red Lion. That ticked me off. How, I wondered, can one work in the Red Lion State Police barracks, with a stone lion outside painted red, and not know about Red Lion? If I were assigned to such a place, I would find out about Red Lion in the first twenty-four hours or die.

The state policemen seemed more interested in me than in Red Lion, and I began to think it might have been a mistake to enter their precincts. One of them asked suspiciously, "What's the matter with your legs?" and when I told him about biking across

Burlington County his eyes narrowed, as if he thought biking the county instead of doing what one was supposed to be doing—whatever that was—was immoral, possibly even illegal. He kept staring at me, trying to read me for . . . what? Clues to some crime? I became more and more uncomfortable. Finally, he shook his head and returned to his desk; I beat a retreat.

Across the circle was the Red Lion Diner, and I went in and had a marvelous breakfast: eggs, pancakes, bacon, home fries, juice, coffee. Breakfast is my favorite meal. I could have breakfast three meals a day. But the waitress couldn't help me out with Red Lion either. "It's just a name," she said matter-of-factly.

Does the loneliness of a solitary trip make finding out about something like Red Lion important? After all, in the Pine Barrens, place names are often peculiar: Double Trouble, Ong's Hat, Hog's Wallow. Still, after breakfast, when I phoned Phil to see if everything was set for Sunday's water portion of the trip, I mentioned Red Lion. He was about to depart for the firehouse, but he said "Hold it" and put down the phone. I could hear what sounded like piles of books being moved about. Soon Phil returned with a book called *Forgotten Towns of New Jersey,* which had a little chapter on Red Lion. "It says here some guy wounded a mountain lion. His gun jams, so he grapples with the lion. By the time the lion's dead it's covered with blood—its own and the man's. That's why they call the place Red Lion."

"But how come nobody around here knows this story?" I asked.

"Come on," Phil said, "You know how it is with local legends. Everybody's interested in them but the locals."

I was still stiff when I clambered onto my bike and painfully pedaled down Route 206, consoling myself with the thought that at least I was getting an early start. I would need it: I had covered only twenty-one miles the first day; I now faced forty-six.

But there would be few historical distractions on this second day. Two miles south of Red Lion circle, Carranza Road veered off Route 206 and headed into the wilderness. The only things to look at now were stunted pines and dwarf oaks and sand roads wandering off into the bush. In places the sand drifted over the paved road, so I had to be careful not to skid. For five miles I saw nothing: not a car, not a person. Then, with no advance notice, I pulled up at a four-way stop: downtown Tabernacle.

"Nice day for January," a woman with her gray hair pulled back in a bun called to me from the porch of what looked like the town's one store.

"It sure is," I said.

"Yep," the woman said.

"Yep," I replied, trying to be agreeable.

I waited a few moments to see if another topic would occur to either of us. After those lonely miles, I sure felt like talking with someone. But when the woman said "yep" again, I figured our conversation had already peaked and I might better continue on my way.

At a sign announcing Wharton State Forest, I passed the first of many lovely streams. These copper-colored waterways meander through the Pine Barrens, taking their time reaching the sea. They bubble out of the sand with water so pure it's drinkable on the spot. At the very center of the eastern megalopolis, in the most densely populated and environmentally degraded state in the nation, I stopped at a creek called Roberts Branch and, reaching down with my cupped hand, quaffed some of its icy goodness.

A few miles down the road I came to the Carranza Memorial. This is the tribute to Mexico's Lindbergh, Emilio Carranza, who crashed here July 13, 1928, on his return from a goodwill trip to New York. Standing at a desolate spot in the Pines, the monument, with its inverted Aztec eagle and legend in both Spanish and English, is strange and haunting, especially if one hasn't seen but one living soul for several hours—and if, as it turns out, the pavement quits just past the monument and all there is now is a rutted sand road.

I had already made thirteen miles that morning, and it was only 9:30, but now my progress slowed markedly. There were times when I had to get off the bike and walk as my wheels sank into the sand. At one point I took a spill, thinking as I went over the handlebars: if I break my leg here, I may freeze before anyone finds me.

But nature is soft in the Pines, and the very sands that threw me off the bike cushioned my fall. Remaining where I fell—the Pine Barrens being a place where you can sit in the middle of the road without worrying overly much about getting run over—I examined the map and saw that while the blue line of my road narrowed just past the Carranza Memorial, it thickened again some three miles farther on. If I could get to that point, I might soon be on pavement again.

Half an hour later I reached a fork in the road. My map showed the thick line going off to the right, but the road to the left was wider and had some remnants of paving. Slavishly, I followed the road to the right, because—well, aren't maps always correct?

Not in the Pines.

I had heard how easy it is to get lost in the Pine Barrens. Two hundred yards farther along, the sand drifted over the road in dunes. Then, what was left of the road split into three roads, paths really, along one of which a large deer, antlers and all, stood looking at me. The deer did it. I decided to return to the fork and pick up the other road. And pray.

Three miles down that semipaved road some ancient yellow lines appeared on the cracked asphalt. This was encouraging. A mile farther, a faded stop sign loomed before me. Civilization! Everything was going to be fine, I said to myself as I turned right onto Route 563 and pedaled south.

Enjoying the speed and the absence of sand pulling at my wheels, I saw that I was now in cranberry country. Square, shallow lakes lined both sides of the road, Jersey's version of rice paddies, with sluice gates between them and pumps on the dikes. There were occasional houses now. One had a sign affixed to it offering "Welding"; another had a red and white barber pole in the front yard. Seven miles of country road on 563, and then I picked up Route 679 for another seven. Just short of New Gretna, the last town in the county, I joined Route 9.

Only this wasn't Bruce Springsteen's Route 9; there were no cages to be sprung from around here. I had counted on finding lodging and dinner on Route 9, remembering how farther north the highway is wall-to-wall motels and fast food. But here Route 9 is a quiet rural road.

I inquired at the general store in tiny New Gretna and was told I could find what I needed south of the Mullica River on Route 9. Bummer. The Mullica divides Burlington County from Atlantic County, and I had hoped, purist that I am, to make the trip entirely within Burlington. But I had a bigger problem: Route 9 briefly disappears into the Garden State Parkway at New Gretna. There was no way across the river except via the Garden State Parkway bridge, and surely bicycles weren't allowed on the Parkway. Not till now, anyway.

Outside New Gretna, with night coming on, I swung with Route 9 onto the ramp of the Parkway, joining for two-and-a-half miles an alien world of speeding vehicles. Luckily, there were no tollbooths where I entered and exited the Garden State, and no police appeared. Luckily, too, there was a shoulder lane—though this shrank to two feet on the bridge itself. Cars passed inches from me, but the danger was compensated for by the vista beyond the bridge rail: a vast, dim world of water and marshes as far as the eye could see. It looked like the place *Prince of Tides* was filmed. Tomorrow I'd be out there.

Sunday morning, I recrossed the Garden State Parkway bridge into Burlington County and met Phil as we had agreed—near New Gretna at an abandoned oyster shack on the Bass River. I don't know how Phil knew about this place, but he did. When I pedaled up, he tossed my bike into the back of his van without so much as a hello. He already had the two sea kayaks on the ground, ready for launching. They were long, heavy vessels made of fiberglass, nothing like the little canvas kayaks you see guys in helmets doing flips in on *Wide World of Sports.*

In his black wet suit, Phil looked like one of the bad guys in *Star Wars.* He checked my clothes—the long johns, the gloves, the great French windbreaker—and said, "Get rid of that stuff." Phil handed me a wet suit and booties and the neoprene skirt that would attach me to the kayak and make a watertight seal around my body.

"I'll freeze to death," I said.

"No way," Phil said. "Those Eskimos know what they're doing."

"I'll drown. The kayak will flip over and I'll be locked into it upside down." Phil showed me how you released the neoprene skirt in an emergency, but I wasn't entirely reassured.

Getting into a wet suit is like pulling a bathing cap onto your whole body. Parts stick, especially some parts that might best not be mentioned here, and it seems impossible all of you will get inside. Then, when you're finally in, you're so snug you can hardly walk. Phil showed me how to insert my hands into the pogies, the watertight gloves that were velcroed around the eight-foot, double-bladed kayak paddle.

We pushed off into the Bass River. The sea kayaks skimmed over the water, and in no time we had covered the mile to Doctor Point, where the Bass flows into the vast, wave-capped estuary of the Mullica. The Mullica begins as a quiet Pine Barrens stream, no bigger than the one where I stopped for a drink the day before, but now it was a big river, tidal and mostly salt water. The main channel was a mile wide, with countless secondary channels coursing among the low marshgrass islands. These islands were more like great patches of mud than real islands; they were treeless and couldn't have been more than two feet above sea level.

"They call this the meadows," Phil said.

"Like the Meadowlands up near New York?" I asked.

"Yeah, except they only started to use that fancy word Meadowlands when Giants Stadium was built. When I was growing up, the North Jersey marshes were called the meadows too."

In front of us a great island of mud and grasses blocked our path. Phil consulted his charts. There was a narrow strait, ominously named Blood Ditch, separating the island from the left bank. Why *Blood Ditch*? I wondered. Had something terrible happened here? Was it about to happen again? But if we could get through Blood Ditch, it would save two miles of paddling around the island, so we decided to chance it, and although the current in the strait was turbulent, we made it.

Now we faced a still wider river, and, with no protection from the marshes, the stiff ocean wind blew salt spray in our faces. We paddled due east, shortcutting across the bends in the river, heading toward the ocean. Phil's charts showed that just to the south was Leed's Point, where, according to legend, Mother Leeds gave birth to her thirteenth child, the famed Jersey Devil. This horned, hoofed, flying creature—New Jersey's own bigfoot or Loch Ness monster—has been inhabiting these dank precincts ever since, the only resident except for an occasional pirate.

More recently, this inaccessible area has become the final resting place for more than one New Jersey murder victim. Indeed, Phil and I later learned that a few days before we made our way through it, the kidnapper-murderers of Exxon executive Sidney Reso had deposited his body in this woeful locale. As if to hint at that grisly crime, the landscape became ever more forlorn, almost frightening.

It nonetheless had a curious beauty, augmented, for me, by the likelihood that not a living soul was enjoying it that day except ourselves. No homeless guy was going to greet Phil and me at the end of *this* trip, that was for sure; there weren't even any homes. What there was was nothing, just the low, miserable mud. Phil didn't say anything, but I sensed he was as much in awe of this strange marsh world as I was.

After two more miles of hard paddling, Phil checked the charts and announced that we were at the entrance to Great Bay, where Burlington, Ocean, and Atlantic counties meet and the ocean begins. "This is the end of Burlington County," Phil said. "Satisfied?"

"Not quite," I answered. Before beginning the long, arduous paddle back to the van, I wanted to actually set foot on the last piece of Burlington County land, so we steered over to the left bank.

We found the spot, which is where Ballanger Creek—originating far to the north in some cranberry bogs—empties into the sea. We paddled up to the tiny spit of land at the mouth of the creek, and I asked Phil, "What's this place called?"

Phil consulted his map and said, disappointedly, "No name."

"Well then," I said, "you're in luck." Unfastening my neoprene skirt, I stepped out of the kayak onto the muck that passed for land thereabouts. The marshland sucked at my booties. The spot was desolate and slimy and loathsome. There were shards of paper-thin ice in the low areas, and it felt colder standing up in the wind. "I hereby name this place Phil Herbert Point," I shouted.

"Thanks," Phil said, drawing his index finger up toward his mouth and making a retching noise.

The towers of Atlantic City sparkled like Oz ten miles south down the coast. And to the west, with the sun setting behind it, was the Garden State Parkway bridge, the same bridge I'd crossed twice on my bicycle, now filled with elephantine tour buses racing nose-to-tail toward those very towers. Aboard, no doubt, were hundreds of crazed old folks just itching to get their Dixie cups and quarters and start feeding the slots. "I bet that's the most traveled bus route in the United States," Phil said.

I kept staring down the coast. Wouldn't it be something, I thought, to arrive in Atlantic City in these sea kayaks? Pull up on the beach like Navy Seals, mount the boardwalk, and stride into a casino in our wet suits, carrying our double-bladed paddles? Liberate the place?

I shared my fantasy with Phil. "Nah," he said. "It wouldn't work. We'd show up in Atlantic City like this and they'd think we're the stage show."

Phil looked over at me. I must have had a long face, because he said, "Okay, some other trip. For now, let's just get out of here. My ass has started to freeze to this kayak."

PART THREE

PHILADELPHIA

Chop-shop Capital

Philadelphia is a handsome city, but
distractingly regular.

CHARLES DICKENS, *AMERICAN NOTES*

Living in New Jersey, one feels the magnetic pull not only of
New York but of Philadelphia. New Jersey is the most densely
populated American state, but it is without cities of consequence,
so Philadelphia is South Jersey's metropolis as New York is
North Jersey's. Benjamin Franklin once wrote, "New Jersey is
like a barrel tapped at both ends." Philadelphia is the other tap.

It is, nonetheless, very different from New York. Philadelphia
is colonial, quiet, low-rise; it produces patrician leaders with
names like Thatcher Longstreth and Richardson Dilworth. Philadelphia is a more livable, a "kinder, gentler" city than New York;
you can still find a place to park. People move more slowly
through Philadelphia's streets; they seem less anxious, perhaps
less ambitious. You don't see so many crazy people in Philadelphia nor smoking limos like those which crowd the streets of
Manhattan.

New York is the capital of the world, while Philadelphia, were
it not for its eighteenth-century architecture, might be mistaken
for Des Moines. W. C. Fields once proposed a contest with a
first prize of one week in Philadelphia; second prize, two weeks.
S. J. Perelman weighed in with a not dissimilar remark. "Philadelphia," he said, "is sometimes known as the City of Brotherly
Love, but more accurately is the City of Bleak November After-
noons."

It was certainly bleak when I began my walk across Philadelphia, but it was March, not November—St. Patrick's Day to be exact; and it was morning. The skies were pewter gray, and I felt just as gray—somewhat bored and apprehensive. I wasn't sure why I was doing this. Was it out of what Emerson called "a foolish consistency"? I had walked New York, so I'd best walk Philadelphia too?

Perhaps my malaise was due to the fact that, by the time of the Philadelphia walk, I had decided to write this book and now was no longer experiencing adventure for adventure's sake. I had an ulterior purpose: looking for material. In the Introduction I write about how I wanted to be, in some measure, the hero of my own life. In writing about my adventures, was I now trying to be the hero of other people's lives?

I felt false somehow, a sellout. The bleakness I experienced on the Philadelphia walk, then, was not that city's fault. I have been in Philadelphia on many occasions and found it charming, so if I tended on my hike through the city to focus on that which was disagreeable, and felt less joy in urban adventure, it was because of a bleakness of the spirit and not of the terrain.

———

I had decided to traverse Philadelphia as I had earlier traversed Manhattan, only there wasn't one street, like Broadway, to take. And since Philadelphia spreads out over the land, isn't confined to an island, doesn't perceptibly descend from a height to the sea, my walk across it would not be so driven by geography. It would have more of a desultory aspect than my Manhattan hike. I would simply diagonal across Philadelphia from its Bucks County border, pass through the center of town, and continue on out to its southwestern extreme at the international airport.

Poquessing Creek, a tired, littered stream with eroded banks, is not one of Philadelphia's major waterways, but it is the northeast boundary of the city and the place where I began. Patricia had driven me down to the city line with our son, Joshua, then four years old, along for the ride. When I got out of the car, Joshua said, "Where are you going?"

"I'm going to walk across Philadelphia," I said.

"Why?" Joshua said.

I didn't know what to say. As the car U-turned and headed back to New Jersey, Joshua looked worriedly out at me through the back window.

I nearly missed Poquessing Creek amidst the collection of roadside eateries and motels clustered about it—not to mention the distraction of the X-rated movie house, which that day was offering a triple feature: *Lip Service, Sizzling Seniors,* and *Eager Beavers.* The "Welcome to Philadelphia" sign assured me as to my whereabouts, but what was I to make of the huge legend a bit farther on, painted on a Roosevelt Boulevard overpass, that said, "God Lied to Me"?

To whom had God lied, and did this person still feel that way? Was there not something ominous about being welcomed to a city and immediately told that God had lied to one of its citizens?

Roosevelt Boulevard, despite such signs and being named for the ebullient Teddy Roosevelt, is dull—all nondescript row houses with pleated aluminum awnings and with a prodigious number of Burger Kings and weed-filled vacant lots where deer occasionally feed. More than once I've read in the Philadelphia newspapers of deer crashing through somebody's front window on Roosevelt Boulevard. Deer aren't supposed to come through windows in cities, but on Roosevelt Boulevard they do.

I soon quit Roosevelt and got on Frankford Avenue, which has no deer but a great deal more urban vitality—Palm Reading by Sister Ruth, the Hercules Restaurant, Original Bernie's Cancellation Shoes, lots of ethnic food stores, and, straight out of *The Great Gatsby,* a billboard with the giant eyes of Dr. M. Falkenstein, optometrist.

At the bottom of the hill where Frankford meets the elevated train, a Kresge's five-and-ten-cents store was loudly blaring "Guantanamera" and there was a sprinkling of Philadelphia's peculiar sidewalk Ad-A-Benches, one offering "Free Foot Facts on Tape, 547-7800."

I didn't expect to require any "foot facts" this trip. My feet were wrapped in Moleskin left over from the Route 22 hike two years before, and I had these leather inserts in my boots as a hedge against the tendinitis that had so marred my Manhattan walk and the raft race.

I got them from a podiatrist I had consulted somewhat apprehensively a month before in an attempt at avoiding the foot pain of earlier urban hikes. I had never been to a podiatrist and thought of them right along with alchemists, phrenologists, and other quacks. Dr. Carlson's waiting room walls were decorated with charts of what looked like dissected feet, and the infirmities exhibited by his other patients were equally unreassuring. Just after I arrived, a man clumped into the office dragging one foot behind him. Down the hall I could see Carlson using what looked like pruning shears on an old woman's horny yellow toenails.

The nurse told me to immerse my feet in what looked like a mini-Jacuzzi. I told her there was nothing wrong with me, that I was just there for advice, but she said, in the tone of a baby-talking nursery school teacher, that it was important to soften my feet "for doctor." This eminence soon appeared, sat opposite me, and, taking my wet feet onto his white-coated lap, turned them this way and that and stroked them ever so gently. I guess if you're into feet, you're into feet.

Dr. Carlson told me my feet were "pronated inward." This horrified me, but he said most people's feet are pronated and it doesn't matter except when walking great distances, especially on hard city surfaces and highways—exactly what I do. He took casts of my feet and prescribed orthotics, the leather inserts, to force me to put my feet down straight when I walked.

No doubt they did, but shortly into the Philadelphia hike my knees ached worse than my Achilles tendons ever had; the orthotics were forcing my legs to bow out like a cowboy's. At the next Ad-A-Bench, I sat down, removed the orthotics from my boots, and slipped them into my back pockets. To this day they sit unused on the shelf in my clothes closet.

Next to the bench was a brick building housing Norman's Bath Boutique, and just above the garbage cans in the wide alley alongside Norman's was a corroded bronze plaque that read:

Erected by the People
  of Frankford
To Mark The Site of An Arch
Where on Behalf of the Citizens
And Assisted by a Choir of
Twenty-Four Young Ladies
General Isaac Worrell
  welcomed
General Marquis de Lafayette
  September, 1824

I wondered whether Norman's customers ever noticed the plaque and, if they did, whether their reactions fulfilled the tender hopes of those who had placed it there. A delivery truck pulled into the alley, and I asked the driver what he knew of the plaque. "Wasn't Lafayette some French guy?" he said. Opined his assistant: "All's I know is the country is filling up with these illegals."

The hill I had come down was a welcome interruption of the otherwise unrelievedly flat terrain. Most of Philadelphia's 129 square miles are a coastal plain more typical of New Jersey and Delaware than of mountainous Pennsylvania. The city averages barely one hundred feet above sea level and was once largely under the ocean, as workmen digging the subways who found sharks' teeth could attest; at its lowest point, the marshlands of Southwest Philadelphia, one can still encounter quicksand.

Frankford Avenue now carried me down into the Kensington neighborhood, which reminds one of Belfast, Northern Ireland— gritty, run-down, working-class white, embattled. The brick row houses are dingy, with busted marble stoops. Signs in store windows offer The Paralyzer, an aerosol tear gas.

Suddenly I understood why the skies were so dark. It began to snow, first a few small flakes, then many large ones. The wind came up, blowing the rapidly increasing snow into my face with such intensity that I could not see and could barely catch my breath. In mid-March, wearing nothing but jeans and a windbreaker, I was walking in a blizzard.

Through a break in the curtain of snow I spotted McGinty's

Tavern and managed to pry the door open against the wind. I brushed the snow off my hair and clothes and decided to have lunch. Corned beef and cabbage and Irish soda bread were being served in honor of the holiday, and there was even green beer available.

Though it was a weekday and during working hours, McGinty's was packed with people, and a carnival atmosphere prevailed. A wizened man of indeterminate age was telling all who would listen that he was the 1943 pinball champion of Philadelphia. I sat at the bar and ordered lunch. On the next stool, a big, blond woman, a tattoo with the simple legend "Willie" emblazoned on that part of her right breast available for inspection, was shouting above the din, "So I said to him, 'I don't care if you're Mick, Polack, or American. I keep a shotgun by the front door and a .45 by the back. You just *try* getting in. Nothing would make me happier than to blow your head off.' "

She turned and looked at me. "You think that's funny or somethin'?" she said.

"What?"

"You think that's funny?"

It's possible I had been smiling at her story. I wasn't smiling now. "No," I said, "I don't think that's funny."

"Whatya, some kind of fancy college guy or something? You think your shit doesn't smell?"

"I. . . ."

"You think that's funny, this is what you can do," she said, thrusting her hand in front of my face with the middle finger raised. Clearly, I thought, Philadelphia, like New York, has more than one kind of wildlife.

This incident put a damper on the enthusiasm I often entertain for walking through cities, meeting "the people," and fancying myself one of them. I was definitely not one of the people in McGinty's, and the woman with the tattoo had told me so. I ate my lunch more quickly than I had planned.

When I emerged from the dark cave of McGinty's, it was as if the snow had never happened. The sun was out, the air warm, and spring had returned. I continued along a sparkling Frankford

Avenue, which now angled toward the Delaware River into Center City. Center City, which is what Philadelphians call their downtown, is a peninsula, a tongue of land bordered by the Delaware River on the east, the Schuylkill River on the west, and the confluence of the two on the south. William Penn laid out Philadelphia where the Delaware and Schuylkill are closest—guaranteeing a city with not one but two waterfronts. Thus, while Center City is not, like Manhattan, an island, it is just as much under the influence of its neighboring waters.

In the shadow of the bright blue Ben Franklin Bridge, at the corner of Front and Vine, I stopped to rest and watched a raft of ruddy ducks, who seemed to inhabit the cove created by two abandoned piers, struggle against the incoming tide. Although Philadelphia is ninety miles from the sea, the ocean visits twice every twenty-four hours, when five-foot tides sweep up the Delaware, salting the river and causing it temporarily to change direction.

It is always thrilling to encounter natural forces at work in the city, but the sun was going down and I needed a place to sleep. Easier said than done. Every hotel I came to as I walked away from the river and past Independence Hall and the striking colonial buildings of the historic district was either full, frightfully expensive, or run-down.

In the frightfully expensive category was the onetime Bellevue Stratford, now not only elegantly refurbished but renamed from the days when it became identified with a new human calamity: Legionnaires' disease. When it was later proven that the virulent virus that killed twenty-nine American Legion conventioneers in 1976 was harbored in the hotel's air conditioning system, this confirmed my long-held conviction that there is something ultimately unhealthy, if not immoral, about air conditioning. My wife, champion of the great indoors, and I have discussed this idea of mine on more than one hot summer night.

Patricia says: "Why are you so austere, so in control? Live a little."

I respond: "Anyone who sets out to canoe to New York or

walk across New Jersey had better be austere and in control or he won't make it."

She says: "Well, if you're so tough, how come you always want to use my car in the summer?" Patricia's car has air conditioning.

I respond: "A moral lapse."

But I'm serious about trying to be in control of my life. If I were to have an operation I'd want local anesthesia and to be awake. When I fly I'm always happier in small planes, no matter how much they bounce around the sky. I can see the guy who's driving it, and if he isn't worried neither am I. Aboard big planes—with their artificial air and artificial music and closed cockpit doors; is anyone actually in there?—I feel anesthetized and utterly unable to influence my fate, a little like those unsuspecting legionnaires in their poisonous, air conditioned hotel.

I finally found a room in the Hotel Apollo, at 19th and Arch, price $49.99. I soon concluded the former Bellevue Stratford wouldn't have been such a bad idea after all. I'm not sure what I expected for my $49.99, but surely a room with a towel more absorbent than a starched shirt; a television set with more colors than pink and green; a water glass. One especially desires such amenities when traveling as light as I was; I wasn't even carrying a toothbrush, planned to keep my teeth clean with some Dentine that was in my pocket.

When I hiked downstairs—the elevator wasn't working—and asked for a water glass the desk clerk took me into his confidence. He winked and whispered, "They keep stealing them on us." I wondered who "they" were. He made a grand gesture of handing me a plastic cup and, as I mounted the stairs, called after me enthusiastically, "Enjoy!" Only when, back in my room, I raised the cup to drink and water dribbled down the front of my shirt did I discover the cup was cracked.

———————

Breakfast the next morning largely made up for the hotel. At the corner of Chesnut and 19th I encountered The Donut Inn, where I sat at the counter and, for $2.09, had orange juice, two eggs, home fries, toast, coffee, and something called scrapple. I thought scrapple was a word game, but here I was eating an indeterminate, meaty substance the short-order cook had cut from a loaf, dusted with flour, and dropped sizzling onto the griddle atop a ladleful of grease. "What is this stuff?" I asked him.

"Scrapple," he said.

"Yes, but what's it made of?"

"Irving," the short-order cook called out to the man who stood stone-faced by the cash register, "tell this gentleman about scrapple."

Irving sprang into action. "Scrapple," he said with a shrug, "is . . . scrapple."

Would inquiring further be considered bad manners in The Donut Inn? I was about to give up the subject as a lost cause when the man on the next stool said quietly, "Pigs' lips and assholes."

"What?" I asked astonished.

"Discarded pig parts. Everything but the squeal."

Philadelphia has other examples of regional cuisine, if this is not too fine a term for scrapple—which, by the way, I ceased eating immediately. The cheesesteak sandwich, greasy with onions, is a Philadelphia delicacy. So is the salt pretzel—well, not the pretzel itself but the way it is eaten. I learned about this after my visit to City Hall.

After breakfast I walked by Philadelphia's statuary-encrusted, Second Empire–style City Hall, the most impressive in America, the one institution in Philadelphia that dwarfs its New York counterpart. Next to Philadelphia's City Hall, New York's would look like a dollhouse. The largest masonry structure in the world— larger than St. Peter's in Rome—Philadelphia's City Hall squats like some great feudal castle in the metropolis's central square, leaving no question as to where power resides in the city.

One senses this not only in the massiveness of the structure but in all the whispered conversations taking place along its stone corridors and behind its smoky glass doors. Much more than in New York, power is centralized in Philadelphia. When Frank Rizzo was mayor, he commented on the CIA-sponsored, ill-fated

1961 Bay of Pigs invasion in Cuba by saying, "It would have been different if they'd sent in the Philadelphia police." When the MOVE cult refused to be extricated from their row house, Mayor Wilson Goode dispatched a helicopter with a bomb, and the result was the annihilation of an entire square block. Many New Yorkers do not even know where City Hall is; *everyone* in Philadelphia knows.

I wanted to get to the top of City Hall so as to see the whole city at once. Easier said than done. First I had to make my way through the advocates for various causes ringing the building, including two competing evangelists, each with his loudspeaker system. "Jesus!" one cried plaintively. "What does *he* know about Jesus?" the other shouted from across the square. Then I had to take a combination of stairs, an escalator, an elevator, and yet another elevator—a real rickety, slow one—to the top, with delays at each level.

Until recently, City Hall was the tallest building in Philadelphia. There had been an understanding that no building might surpass the Quaker hat atop the head of the giant statue of William Penn that crowns the tower. This understanding had now been violated several times, especially by two particularly brutal-looking blue towers, but the view, as I stood at William Penn's noble feet, still fulfilled my hopes. The city was laid out before me like a diorama. I could see the terrain over which I had walked the day before and my itinerary for the rest of that day, even out to where planes skimmed in over the misty far reaches of the city as they approached the airport.

Descending to the street, I encountered a Greek salt pretzel vendor, who said he had been selling his wares on Walnut Street ever since immigrating to the United States twenty years before. "A lot or a leetle?" he asked.

"A lot or a little what?" I responded. Was one expected in Philadelphia to buy several pretzels at a time?

He looked at me quizzically and said something that sounded like mustache, only he meant mustard. That's when I learned of a key gastronomic difference between Philadelphia and New York: Philadelphians eat their salt pretzels with mustard. Only one hundred miles away, New Yorkers would freeze in horror at such a prospect. It was nice to discover that all of America hadn't yet become McDonald's, that some regionalism was still alive on Walnut Street in Philadelphia.

Walnut Street. Philadelphia's main avenues are virtually all named for trees, for the Quakers considered naming streets for people unseemly if not blasphemous. In all, 150 of Philadelphia's streets are named for native plant life, beginning with Acorn and going all the way to Verbena. Such street names contribute to Philadelphia's small-town feeling. There is a world of difference not only in scale but in tone between Broadway in New York and Walnut, Chestnut, and Pine in Philadelphia.

Philadelphians like to say they have more trees than any city in the world and greater variety as well. The variety might be explained by the city being where North and South meet. Philadelphia is, for example, both the northern terminus of the Carolina hemlock and the southern terminus of the Canadian hemlock. Philadelphians take as a matter of course the meteorological phenomenon of snow in the northeastern part of the city simultaneous with rain in the southwestern. Indeed, as I was to learn in a phone conversation with the United States Weather Service a few days later, it was raining at the airport at precisely the time I experienced the miniblizzard on St. Patrick's Day.

After leaving City Hall, I trudged down Broad Street for several miles. Increasingly, the names and bell plates on the row houses became Italian—Mesina, Giordano, Esposito. This was South Philadelphia, scene of the *Rocky* movies. Statues of saints sprouted in front yards, and there was a sprinkling of busybodies on the top floors—systems of mirrors whereby you can see who's at the front door from upstairs without showing yourself.

I was staring at one of these busybodies, above Delvecchio's Grocery, when the proprietor came outside and asked, in what, at first, seemed a good-natured way, "You planning to blow the place up? Why not? We got insurance."

"What?" I said.

"Go ahead," he said, showing a lot of teeth, "be my guest.

Only don't rob me, okay? You blow up the place we both go to Florida on the insurance, but rob me and we don't get *caca*."

"What are you talking about?" I said, but he abruptly went inside and I decided to just move on. In Philadelphia, people are local, territorial. Everyone knows everyone else, and since Delvecchio didn't know me, and thought I might be casing his grocery store, he challenged me. At least, I think that's what happened.

The incident made me feel a little as I had in McGinty's Tavern: like a stranger. New York is a world city, so everyone's on an equal footing, everyone's a stranger. New York doesn't have institutions like Philadelphia's Mummers—secret societies of grown men parading about in feathers and bangles and beads each New Year's Day. Philadelphia is a large small town. People either belong or they're strangers.

At the corner of South Broad and Passyunk was the chrome and glass Melrose Diner, where I had some Danish and coffee. I needed the respite. I was shook-up from the conversation at Delvecchio's Grocery, and I was about to begin the last, and least eagerly anticipated, part of my trip. Coming in from Philadelphia's northeastern outskirts the day before, I had felt some excitement as I approached Center City. Now I felt dispirited. It seemed stupid to be wilfully abandoning the relative glamour of downtown for Passyunk Avenue and the grim further outskirts of Philadelphia.

Passyunk is the Delaware Indian word for level place, which certainly described the terrain thereabouts: level and boring. Approaching the Schuylkill, one might be tempted to add *ugly* to the list. Upriver, I knew, genteel oarsmen in tennis shoes and whites train for the Olympics in one-man sculls, but here the river was characterized by the hideous industry on its banks and, especially for me, by the perilously rusted-out walkway of the iron bridge I was now attempting to cross. On the other side of the river was Eastwick, the largest and most sparsely settled section of Philadelphia. Eastwick is where yellow fever victims were quarantined during the epidemics of the eighteenth century, and it looked as if it might still be appropriate for such a purpose today.

This wasn't what William Penn had in mind when he envisioned Philadelphia as a "greene countrie towne." The largest oil refining complex on the East Coast stretched as far as the eye could see, while in the foreground was an endless array of auto junkyards, each with its colorful name. There was Smashy's and Spanky's and Ajax Late Model Auto Parts / "Ask for Pete" and Louie's Smart Parts. It looked like your car wouldn't remain intact half an hour if you made the mistake of parking outside one of these places. Indeed a few weeks after my hike, I was in my dentist's office glancing at an article on car theft in *Time* magazine, and it referred to Passyunk Avenue as "the chop-shop capital of America."

The article didn't mention the ferocious guard dogs—German shepherds, Doberman pinschers, pit bulls—who acted, as I passed, like no one on foot had gone by on Passyunk Avenue in ten years and were expressing their outrage on the matter. The dogs rushed about inside the chain link fences, persecuting me with their merciless fang-bared barking, as eager to chop me up as their masters were to chop cars.

I found myself thinking about the "God Lied to Me" sign. Was Eastwick what the lie had been about? Or was the lie inherent in my conceit that, by my mere presence, I could liberate even the most deformed urban landscape? Trans-Schuylkill Philadelphia certainly looked deformed to me now—deformed and evil. There were even big For Sale signs posted about in the marsh that ominously boasted "Zoned Least Restrictive."

Passyunk took a curve, and now the street was called Essington. A sidewalk had been built along Essington, but it was obvious no one ever used it, for it was as overgrown as a two-thousand-year-old Roman road. The rank vegetation emerging through its cracks brushed against me uncomfortably and went up my pants legs. It was easier to walk in the street.

I heard a vehicle approaching behind me. I kept walking, trying to ignore it, but it pulled alongside, and then red, white, and blue lights flashed. An amplified voice challenged: "Whadya doing out here?"

"Just walking."

"Why?" the voice in the police cruiser bellowed. That was the same question my son Joshua had asked.

Why indeed? I thought. "I'm walking across the city. I'm trying to get to the city line."

Without another word, but with a look of severe disapproval on his face, the officer made a screeching U-turn and headed back to town. It appeared that even he, hermetically sealed in his mobile fortress, didn't care to go any farther along Essington Street.

Near the airport, Essington made a sharp turn to the right that wasn't on my street map, but old Essington was still there, so I took it because it seemed a more direct route. A reed marsh was encroaching on the abandoned Essington, and into it the concrete edges of the street were breaking off in chunks. There was garbage everywhere. A large brown Norway rat, oily and bushy, scampered across the road, looked at me, and continued on its way.

Seeing the rat in the near dark gave me the creeps. I wished I could have overcome my prejudice and appreciated it as just another life-form sharing the city. I tried telling myself that if animals survive in the city, there's a decent chance for people, but that isn't what I felt. What I felt was disgust. Maybe it was a combination of things: not only the rat but the assault by the tattooed blond in McGinty's; the paranoid conversation with Delvecchio; the vicious dogs along Passyunk Avenue; and, of course, the "God Lied to Me" sign. Whatever it was, I was fast learning I wasn't as much the square-jawed Mark Trail of an urban outdoorsman as I pretended to be.

In conceiving the idea for this book, I had ambitiously hoped I could find adventure, just as satisfying as the traditional kind, not where no one has been but where no one wishes to go. Now this notion seemed foolish. It occurred to me that there are perfectly good reasons for not going where no one wishes to go. I had also hoped that this book would be a love letter to my much abused land. But I wasn't feeling very loving as I stood among the degraded remains of old Essington Street. I was tired. I wanted to go home.

Yet I was still the same goal-oriented person who got depressed when Phil and I narrowly missed circumnavigating Manhattan. In my place, Phil could have quite happily quit this hike right then and there, and of course Patricia, with no remorse, would have quit the trip, assuming she had ever started it, five minutes after crossing Poquessing Creek the day before, or certainly when it began to snow.

Someday, a circumstance may arrive where the true adventure, given who I am, may be in quitting rather than persisting, but, right now, I couldn't stand having walked this far only to quit. So I plodded on, and soon I was skirting the great chain link perimeter fence of Philadelphia International Airport. It was a strange place to be on foot, what with jet airplanes roaring in over my head one after another like great winged beasts. When I got around the airport, I couldn't find the city limits sign in the dark, but I knew from my map that the airport's far side is Delaware County. So I had made it; I had crossed Philadelphia.

Skirting the perimeter again, I entered the airport terminal, where I felt like a swamp creature amidst the bright lights and hubbub of voices in the cavernous building. There was a half-hour wait for the next bus to Center City, so I bought candy bars and a copy of *People* magazine in the gift shop and found a seat in one of the waiting lounges. I simultaneously gorged on an Almond Joy, a Butterfinger, and the annual cover story in *People* called "The Sexiest Man Alive," disappointed once again to discover that the article was not about me. I was treating myself, nevertheless, after what felt to me then like two days of sensory deprivation. Patricia would be proud of me, I thought. I'm living a little.

Soon I found myself on the bus, seated among bewildered travelers and their belongings, rushing down some of the same streets I had trod foot by foot that very day. My dark mood was lifting. I took a certain satisfaction in knowing that, unlike the travelers who had been flown here from Los Angeles or London, I had walked twenty-six miles across Philadelphia for the privilege of taking that bus.

10 Deliverance

We hoped only to paddle silently through the world.

RAYMOND MUNGO, *TOTAL LOSS FARM*

It was perhaps inevitable that if I had canoed to New York from New Jersey I might someday wish to reverse direction and canoe to Philadelphia. Such a trip would provide a certain symmetry to, and neatly complete, the present cycle of my adventures. It might also help me to recover my enthusiasm for urban adventure after the negative thoughts that dogged me in connection with my walk across Philadelphia.

Patricia was aware of these thoughts. She kept saying, "What's the matter with you?" and when I told her she said, "So what? You're not just a rider; you're a writer."

"Yeah," I said, "but I feel like I'm at a party and, instead of participating, I'm sneaking around taking photographs. I feel dishonest somehow."

"Why? Aren't you telling the truth in the book?"

"Well, mostly. . . . I write what I remember or maybe what I *want* to remember. I probably exaggerate sometimes."

"What else is new?" she said.

A few minutes later she said, "But the book isn't fiction, is it?"

"No," I replied, "but sometimes I think all writing is fiction. It's just that some writing is more fictional than other writing."

"You sound like Orwell," she said. "'All animals are equal but some animals are more equal than other animals.'" Then she put her arm around me and said, "And some animals are *still* more equal."

That cheered me a bit. But it wasn't just writing the book that made me feel vaguely corrupt. That innocent moment long ago when, on a whim, I stopped my car and mounted the hillside above Interstate 287 and lay down under the pines and listened to the roaring of the trucks and the droning of the cicadas now seemed lost to me. I wanted to get back to that hillside. I had felt something important up there. Let me see if I can put it into words: that a virgin landscape can be only pretty; beauty requires some artful intrusion of human works into the landscape. Walden is just a pond; Walden with Thoreau's cabin on it charms the soul.

Would the challenge of traversing the cities and towns and polluted waters between central New Jersey and Philadelphia, even if I did write about it, serve as a kind of purification ceremony and get me back to that hillside? I hoped so.

But was there a water route to Philadelphia, and could I convince Phil Herbert to go with me once more? The last time we spoke he had made a crack: "What's next for you, Michael, snowshoeing through sewers?"

I determined to scout the trip thoroughly before discussing it with Phil—rivers, tides, whatever; I didn't want him bitching about my being an amateur.

I embarked on a day-long expedition by car, some features of which I report here. Clearly, the way out of central New Jersey was via my old friend the Delaware and Raritan Canal—this time canoeing it rather than biking its towpath; and in the opposite direction. But what to do where the canal goes under the Route 1 freeway for a mile or so in Trenton?

Standing alongside the canal at that point, I spotted a line of trees half a mile away. Could there be a river there? My Sunoco road map showed a blue wiggly line to the east that seemed to pass through Trenton. This, I learned, was Assunpink Creek. If it could be followed out to the Delaware, getting to Philadelphia would be all but assured. I looked up Assunpink Creek in James and Margaret Cawley's book *Exploring the Little Rivers of New*

Jersey, but the Cawleys don't mention it. As I was to learn, they may have had good reason not to.

I took a look at portions of the Assunpink on foot and by car. Though lined with debris, it looked passable. But alongside the Amtrak railroad station, a stone's throw from where the Metroliner thunders by on its way to Washington, the creek descends in a rush of water and disappears under Trenton into a dark tunnel. And the gorge at that point is almost vertical, impossible to portage around.

I pulled into the railroad station parking lot. It seemed an indignity to pay for parking in such circumstances, and I told the attendant I would only be a minute; I was checking the tunnel.

"What tunnel?" he said.

"The one the Assunpink goes through?"

"Assun what?" It did not augur well for the viability of the Assunpink and its tunnel if this attendant was utterly unaware of their existence. Nor was I gratified to hear him say, "That'll be $3.75."

I walked the city streets some six hundred yards and found the place where, in the middle of downtown Trenton, the Assunpink emerges. But what was in that tunnel, and could two men in a canoe get through it?

I went to a phone booth and six calls later was connected to the Mercer County Planning Department. "Tell me about that tunnel," I said.

I could hear the man on the other end of the line rustling some charts. "What about it?" he finally said.

"What's in it?"

"It's just a tunnel," he said.

"Yes, but could a canoe get through it? Are there any dangerous animals down there?" Alligators in the New York City sewers might be a myth, but this tunnel was big enough and mysterious enough to be inhabited by any number of creatures.

"We're not responsible," was all the man would say in reply.

Back at the station parking lot I sat thinking and looking down at the rushing water, high above the creek on a pile of abandoned railroad ties. Railroad ties? Of course!

The first tie crashed end over end down the gorge and got hung up in the crotch of a tree at water's edge. The second tie made it to the Assunpink but sank like a stone. Perhaps it was too weighted down with creosote. I rolled some older, lighter ties down the slope. Four of them made it into the river, bobbed to the surface, and promptly charged into the turbulent waters at the mouth of the tunnel. For good measure I threw a large dead tree limb with plenty of branches down into the river. Then I sprinted the six hundred yards to the other end of the tunnel.

Out of breath, I waited. Could they have already gone by? Were they stuck in the tunnel? Ten minutes passed before the first railroad tie emerged into the sunlight, but it was followed in rapid succession by the other three, as if, after years of service to the railroad, the ties had a natural tendency to couple. Three minutes later the tree limb also emerged from the tunnel, some of its branches as high out of the water as our heads would be. Getting through the tunnel in a canoe looked to be scary but possible.

"Piece of cake," I told Phil Herbert when I called to talk him into this new adventure. "A tiny portage over to the Assunpink, a tunnel to go through, and we're in the Delaware."

"What's *tiny*, exactly?"

"Well. . . ."

"And how long did you say that tunnel was?"

I hadn't said. Quickly changing the subject, I asked Phil if he had any floatable flashlights among his gear. He had better than that: helmets with lanterns built into them, left over from his spelunking days. Phil was so eager to use them he forgot all about the portage and the tunnel.

We started our Memorial Day weekend trip as we had the trip to New York—at Phil's garage near Hightstown. The same haul down to the virtually waterless Millstone, the same as-much-by-land-as-by-sea paddle to Lake Carnegie in Princeton. But this time we paddled the yellow canoe up the lake, away from the dam, to where it dwindles into the brook that feeds it at its southern end. Here we portaged the few yards into the Delaware and Raritan Canal and continued smoothly on our way.

We had gone twelve miles, and Phil hadn't complained once, when we reached the Route 1 freeway. "You want to portage where?" Phil asked, genuinely astonished.

"Right over there," I said cheerfully.

"*Right?* You call that *right?*"

Cursing, Phil hefted his end of the canoe and stomped off a few paces, dragging my end through the mud. He turned. "Do I have to carry it by myself?" he said.

We moved along the edges of a cornfield, past a gas station, and past a new condo development. "Almost there," I kept calling.

"Yeah, sure," Phil answered. Huge sweat stains bloomed on the back of his shirt. I could feel the sweat trickling down my body too and wanted to rest but dared not say so.

"Whadya call this river?" Phil, out of breath, asked when we finally reached our destination.

"The Assunpink. George Washington camped along it after the Battle of Trenton."

"Yeah," said Phil, "but when Washington was here the banks weren't nothing but shopping baskets."

Nor, Phil might have added, tires, construction rubble, the remains of a 1953 Hudson, bags of garbage, sheets of plastic, the better part of a bicycle wedged in a tree—one wheel turning aimlessly—paint cans, and a brass bed, half in the river, springs sprung every which way. It would be like canoeing through a flea market. Tattered rags, which must have descended the river high on the spring flood, were wrapped around the branches of trees and fluttered in the wind like pennants, adding a false note of gaiety to the mournful scene.

We got into the river somehow and, as we moved deeper into Trenton, graffiti-covered factories surrounded by razor wire appeared along the banks. Soon we were passing under solid walls of factories on both sides. Most of them were abandoned or boarded up, but some still functioned fitfully; and as the banks got higher and more precipitous it became difficult to avoid the stuff they spilled down on us. A thin pipe extending out over the river from one factory spat steam in explosive gasps. A thicker pipe from another factory emitted a smelly brown liquid that poured down the side of the gorge, leaving a long stain on the rock. "Steer good," Phil said. "That stuff'll peel flesh."

The river became uglier and uglier. The Assunpink was the River Styx, and we were descending into Hades.

But things were about to get worse. Three kids stood high above us at the top of the gorge, looking down impassively. Two of them were maybe ten or eleven, the other about sixteen, but I couldn't see them clearly, for they were silhouetted against the sky. Naively, I waved. Seconds later something seemed to jump out of the water. Could fish live in the Assunpink? Then it happened again. Now something struck the side of the canoe with a loud "pang." It wasn't fish; those kids were throwing rocks at us.

"Hey," I yelled up at them, "cut that out." In response, a small rock glanced off my shoulder, leaving a burning sensation.

I began to steer the canoe in zigzag fashion to make less of a target, but failed to notice some logs sticking out of the river, and we ran aground. Phil got into the water and tried to drag us off. The bow was free, but the stern, where my weight was, held fast. Rocks were raining all around us. A brightly colored object smashed inside the canoe and caromed around crazily. I stepped into the water and swung my paddle menacingly. "You little bastards," I yelled. "Cut that out or I'm coming after you."

This was a vain threat, and they knew it. The gorge was so steep I'd have needed mountain-climbing gear to get out of it. But the rocks stopped temporarily, and Phil pulled the canoe free. Not taking our eyes off the kids, we got into the canoe and pushed off downriver.

The rocks started again. Hunching down in the canoe, we paddled as fast as we could, but the rocks kept coming. The kids were running down the high bank after us, throwing everything they could lay their hands on. "They're crazy," Phil yelled.

Those kids certainly weren't fooling around. They really wanted to hurt us, maybe even brain us. This was especially true of the older one. He wasn't smiling or laughing like the younger boys but had the grim determination of a killer. "You paddle," Phil yelled. "I'll keep my eyes on them."

This strategy worked pretty well. However inefficient it was for only one of us to paddle while the other yelled and stared threateningly, fewer rocks came at us. Those kids were like dogs that quit barking and advancing on you when you stare them down.

But they kept following us. And if Phil turned his back for a moment to help me paddle, rocks pelted us anew.

Then we got lucky. A factory was built right to the edge of the gorge, blocking those malevolent children from coming any farther. A few last rocks showered harmlessly around us, and then the kids were lost to sight. We went another two hundred yards to make sure we were out of range and then steered into the bank, where Phil tied our bow rope to an overhanging tree so we could rest. We were both agitated. I reached in front of me and picked up a number 7 billiard ball and showed it to Phil.

"The guidebook didn't mention the demented natives," he growled.

"Yeah," I replied, "Didn't say anything about this being a 'Hard Hat Only' river either."

"That reminds me," Phil said. "Remember our first trip, the one around Manhattan Island, when I said, 'This could be a lot worse than *Deliverance*'?"

"Yeah, yeah," I said quietly, feeling guilty that I had now exposed Phil to just such danger.

"And remember," Phil continued, "how I said, 'Those guys in *Deliverance* got buggered, and they were just out in the woods'?"

"Yeah," I said, wishing he would change the subject.

"Well," he said, further warming to his theme, "there was a moment when those rocks were hitting us when I'd have settled for getting buggered."

"Glad to know that," I laughed, delighted that the conversation was taking on a light tone after all. "If we meet those kids again, I'll let them know."

"Fuck you," Phil said.

"Nah, nah," I replied. "You're the one who wants to get buggered."

"Well, fuck you anyway," said Phil, releasing our bow rope from the tree.

The Assunpink's current picked us up. Two hundred yards farther we came around a bend, and there, downriver, was the tunnel, black and menacing, the water at its mouth roiled and turbulent. Getting stoned by those junior assassins didn't scare me half as much as the approaching tunnel. Sure, I had checked it out pretty good, but I was terrified something under there would get us anyway. For Phil it was the murderous kids, but for me it was the tunnel from which I sought deliverance.

I glanced at my watch. It was 3:30. I had arranged to phone Ralph Thompson once we had passed through the tunnel. He's my neighbor, the insurance guy who thought the waters around Manhattan would dissolve a canoe and had later warned me about walking on the highway shoulder during my Route 22 expedition. Our understanding was this: if I didn't phone Ralph by 4:30, this meant we were trapped under the city of Trenton and he should launch a rescue.

I'd chosen Ralph for this mission because Patricia and the children were away visiting family in Boston that weekend and because Ralph is such an excruciatingly careful guy. Once a few neighbors and I had wanted to organize a block party, but Ralph was opposed. He said that while police barriers were up on each end, our block would be technically a private street. If, during a foot race, somebody's child tripped on a crack and broke an ankle, we, the neighbors, could be sued.

We went ahead and had the block party anyway. To dissociate himself from the party, Ralph loaded his family into the car and drove away, not returning until dark. I was peeved and didn't talk to Ralph much after that, but he was still my next-door neighbor, and I figured if there was anyone I could rely on when it came to safety, he was the guy.

I thought about being stuck in the tunnel. Klieg lights and television cameras poised at entrance and exit. Microphones floated down to us in plastic bags. Police bullhorns echoing through the dark, minelike recesses of the tunnel: "How long can you hold out in there?" Phil shivering with the cold, beginning to go numb with exposure. The governor arriving on the scene. Newspapers headlining: "Two Men Trapped under City of Trenton." Phil and me heroically emerging from the tunnel days later, leaning on frogmen, our faces blackened, weak but smiling.

Phil snapped me back to the present. "Here we go," he shouted. The current, which increased as we got closer to the narrow tunnel, swept us up, and we rushed down into the abyss.

Despite my fears, the tunnel was the very "piece of cake" I'd cavalierly promised Phil it would be. It was pitch dark, but we moved along as smoothly as if we were on greased rails in the tunnel of love. It was delightfully cool under there, the sound of water echoing off the concrete walls and ceiling. With the current, it was not necessary to paddle, so we got down into the bottom of the canoe; less chance that way of banging heads on a beam or colliding with bats. My eyes gradually grew accustomed to the darkness, and I could now see a pinhole of light far ahead—but nothing else, not even my own hand in front of my face.

As we moved farther along the tunnel I could pick out Phil's form in front of me, silhouetted against the ever-expanding light of the tunnel exit. Several more minutes went by, and then we emerged into the warm sunshine.

"We did it!" I exulted. I had been terrified; now I was giddy with relief.

Phil was not as happy. "Dammit," he said, "we forgot to wear the lantern helmets. The one chance we have to wear those helmets, and we blow it."

"Hey," I replied, "I thought *I'm* the compulsive one."

The Assunpink on this side of the tunnel was in striking contrast to the nightmarish other side. The banks were gentle and clean, lined with cherry trees and flowers and ornate benches. The river was at the center of a little park in which families had spread blankets and were picnicking and playing ball. It was as if we had passed into another country.

Leaving our canoe in the custody of the closest picnicking family, we walked through the park and emerged stiff-legged into downtown Trenton near State and Broad. The golden-domed state capitol was just up the street. "I need a cup of coffee," Phil said.

We found a luncheonette, where Phil ordered coffee and I got into the phone booth to call Ralph. Perfect: it was only 4:05.

Ralph's phone rang and rang. No answer. I joined Phil and had some coffee and Hostess Twinkies and then called Ralph again. No answer. It was 4:18.

I ordered another cup of coffee and went to phone again. Still no answer. It was 4:28. Ralph was supposed to call the rescue squads and frogmen at 4:30. I kept dialing, but no one answered at Ralph's house.

I kept trying to reach Ralph, but when it got to be 5:15, Phil said, "Fuck 'im." Phil was irritated by the delay; he wanted to get on with the trip. Also, he wasn't overly fond of Ralph. Once, when visiting my house, he had met Ralph and said afterward, "Is that guy the complete asshole or what?" We left the luncheonette and went back to the Assunpink.

But my mind wasn't easy. Had Ralph understood 6:30 instead of 4:30? Would he turn the state upside down in an hour when we were out in the Delaware incommunicado? Maybe something had happened to Ralph. There were burglars in his house, and he and his family were tied up and gagged; he knew it was me phoning and prayed I would do something to save them. Or maybe he was home alone and had slipped in the shower and was even now lying in the tub unconscious, the water slowly rising over his face. Or maybe I had mistaken Ralph's phone number and had been dialing incorrectly all this time.

I asked Phil to wait by the canoe, returned to the luncheonette, and called Information. I had the correct phone number. I tried the number again. No answer. I called the police and told them I was afraid something terrible had happened. Would they check Ralph's house? I knew that house. I lived right next to it.

Fifteen minutes later, as instructed, I phoned the police again and was patched through to the radio in the patrol car outside Ralph's house. The officer there, barely controlling his anger, said over a crackling connection that no one was home, the house hadn't been broken into, and he saw nothing amiss when he peered through the windows.

I told him Ralph was supposed to have called the police if I didn't phone him by 4:30, because that meant Phil and I were trapped in a tunnel under the city of Trenton.

"What?" the policeman said.

I tried explaining it again in a simplified manner. I said, "Look, if a Ralph Thompson calls the police and says that a guy named Michael Rockland and another guy, Phil Herbert, are trapped under the city of Trenton, please don't do anything, okay? Don't inform the police in Trenton and don't call the state police, okay? Tell Thompson I called and everything's all right."

"Okay, Mr. Thompson," the policeman said.

"No, no," I said. "*He's* Thompson."

"Then who are you?" the policeman asked.

Our conversation was beginning to sound like that old Abbot and Costello movie routine where Abbot explains baseball to Costello. Any moment I expected the policeman to ask, "Who's on first?"

"Look," I said, "forget the names, okay? Just, if someone calls and says some guys are trapped under the city of Trenton in a tunnel, it isn't true, okay?"

"Okay," the officer said, "nobody's trapped under the city of Trenton in a tunnel."

But he couldn't stop worrying it, couldn't quite leave it alone. His voice took on a confidential tone, like he was auditioning for Peter Falk's *Columbo* role. "Just tell me one thing," he said. "Why am I here checking Thompson's house if he isn't trapped under the city of Trenton? And even if he is trapped under the city of Trenton, why am I checking his house?"

It was hopeless. The conversation continued, but I shall spare the reader further details. I'm not sure I'd even have patience to write them down. Suffice it to say that I soon returned to the river where Phil was angrily pacing up and down by the canoe. I informed him of my further attempts to locate Ralph.

Phil said, "First we don't use the miner's helmets. Then we

waste gobs of time trying to communicate with that asshole neighbor of yours. Didn't I tell you? Fuck 'im."

Still worrying about Ralph but mindful that we had already lost two precious hours, I got in the canoe with Phil, and we pushed off into the placid last half mile of the Assunpink. Ahead, the Delaware loomed, shimmering in the late afternoon sun.

Leaving the tiny river on which we had had so many adventures, we entered a vast water world. The Delaware looked to be half a mile across and, as whitecaps whipped around us, we reached for our life jackets. The tide was going out, just as I had planned. "Hey," Phil yelled, "you're getting the hang of it at last."

We glided under the first of Trenton's bridges, where the current swirled, sucking us toward the pilings. Then we went under another; then a third. One of the bridges had a huge sign, "Trenton Makes, the World Takes." Once that was true. Now half the city was a slum, the other half the state government; and it took.

Our first day's goal had been to make it out to the Delaware, and we had met it. But the sun was going down fast, and we needed a place to camp. Neither the Jersey nor the Pennsylvania side looked hospitable. There were gravel pits, railroad tracks, factories, chemical storage tanks, and rank growth of all kinds. I thought: maybe we can just float along all night like Huck and Jim. But a canoe isn't a raft, and, besides, I was tired and hungry and it was getting chilly on the water.

The ugliness of the banks was briefly broken on the Jersey side by a handsome house with an American flag and a sign that said "Trenton Marina." In the river a small fleet of powerboats bobbed at anchor.

We steered for the dock and, tying the canoe to it, walked up the long yellow gangway. Onshore, a man waited, watching us. He turned out to be the owner of the marina, Roger Stamato, and a nicer guy you'll never meet. Sure we could put up our pup tent in the field beside his house. Sure we could use his phone.

We sat on the ground by the tent and ate a box of Triscuits and a can of Australian corned beef that opened with a key. Phil cut off hunks of the meat with his pocketknife and handed them to me. Stamato had invited us for coffee, so, after eating, we went over to his house just as the last of the light disappeared behind Pennsylvania.

Stamato's living room was fixed up like the inside of a boat, with lots of nautical gear hanging on the walls. Two powerboat owners stood around with steaming coffee mugs. A citizens band radio crackled in the corner, and the television and radio were also on. The next day's weather forecast came on: rain and wind from the south. Nuts!

One of the powerboat owners said the weather didn't need to concern us. "It couldn't be more than five hours' paddle from here to Philadelphia," he said.

"You crazy, Paul?" said the other. They're lucky if they get there in three days, and that's if they don't drown first." So much for informed advice.

I excused myself to use the phone. Dialing Ralph's number, I was startled when it was picked up on the first ring. "Ralph?"

"Yeah."

"You all right?"

"Of course I'm all right. Who's this?"

"Michael." I awaited some acknowledgment of grievous error. An "Oh, no!" or "Keeerist!" or a plea for forgiveness would have been sufficient. I was prepared to be generous.

Nothing.

"Michael who?" Ralph said.

"Michael Rockland!"

"Hey," Ralph said, "how are you, Mike? How come you're phoning instead of knocking on the old door? Something the matter?"

"That's what I'm calling to find out."

Still nothing.

"Ralph, let me ask you something," I said, finally. "Where were you at 4:30 today?"

"Where was I?"

"Yeah?"

"What is this, Mike, 'Twenty Questions'?" Ralph said, becoming irate.

"No, seriously, Ralph, where were you?"

"Me and Lola and the kids were at the beach, that's where I was at 4:30 today. Anything wrong with that?"

"No, Ralph," I said, "nothing at all," and I hung up. Ralph, the great insurance man, the guy who was always counseling caution, had totally forgotten. State Farm hadn't been there like any kind of neighbor, good or otherwise. Had Phil and I gotten stuck under Trenton, we'd have stayed under Trenton forever.

I had tried to do everything right. I had investigated that fearsome tunnel, but unforeseen kids had almost killed us. I had lined up Ralph as a safety fallback, and all that had accomplished was to get Phil mad at me and wreck several hours of our trip. So much for lists and planning, I thought.

I caught a look at myself in the mirror next to the phone. My face was burned, my hair stood out at angles, and I was filthy. But there was a mischievous grin on my mouth, and my eyes looked incredibly blue and shone with a new independence. "You were right about Ralph," I whispered to Phil when I rejoined the little circle in Stamato's living room. "Fuck 'im."

———————

We were out on the river early in the morning. It wasn't raining yet, but the skies looked mean. Once again, the tide was with us, the buoys in the channel leaning out to sea. We slid quickly by the Fairless Steel Works on the Pennsylvania side, an enormous grouping of buildings with broken windows and crumbling smokestacks, silent, a museum of America's onetime industrial might.

Some miles farther on, a large brick house came into view on the Pennsylvania side. "Will you look at the size of that thing?" Phil said. "Must belong to an orthodontist."

It was, in fact, Pennsbury, William Penn's estate, and we decided to do a little tourism. We beached the canoe and were walking up the path to the manor house when a woman in colonial costume came running toward us shouting, "You can't come in here. You have to come through the main gate." She pointed off vaguely inland.

How can we come through the main gate?" I remonstrated. "We arrived by canoe."

"I'm sorry," the woman said, "those are the rules." She suggested we paddle downriver a half mile, walk around the entire property, and buy tickets at the main gate. "We're not set up for people to come in from the river," she said.

"You're not set up for people, period," said Phil.

The woman colored, but she remained adamant. There was nothing to do but beat a retreat and forget Pennsbury. It was difficult to square the magnificence of William Penn's statue atop Philadelphia's City Hall with the pettiness of our treatment at his house, but I quickly forgot the incident, for it had started to rain.

Compounding our troubles, it was now slack tide on the Delaware. We made decent progress, but it wasn't the same as when we rode with the tide. And soon the buoys started leaning upriver, and our forward progress all but ceased. When Phil suggested a tow, I didn't argue.

Incredibly, the first powerboat that came by stopped for us. It was a small blue-and-white fiberglass with a covered cockpit. The name *Linda* was stenciled on the stern. A burly man in his late thirties and his chubby, blond wife looked down on us. They wore identical captain's hats with gold braid and anchors and were so friendly they insisted we ride with them instead of being towed—which was all right with us.

I wanted to show the man, whose name was Buddy, some identification, even though he didn't ask for any. The only thing Phil and I had between us was my Visa card. Buddy looked at it reluctantly and said, "Never use these things myself. If I can't pay cash for something, I don't buy it. Take this boat. There's a V-8 Chevy motor in this baby, and I *own* it." Then he pointed to his wife and said, "Oh, this here's Linda. Same name's the boat."

Buddy got behind the wheel, and the boat took off at terrific speed. Our canoe skipped along on the waves behind us. "Where you headed?" Buddy asked.

"Philadelphia," I said.

"Whydja want to go there for?" Buddy asked, turning serious.

"You know somethin'? I don't need Philadelphia for nothin'. They can take the whole place and shove it. Nothin' but animals down there. The other day they sawed some old lady's arms off. Nothin' but animals in Philadelphia."

"Anybody want a beer?" Linda asked brightly.

We were approaching the Turnpike bridge, and Linda switched on the citizens band radio. "Breaker five," she said, or something like that. "We're in the blue-and-white boat."

"I see you," the box squawked back.

"Who're you talking to?" Phil asked.

"That truck up there." She pointed to an eighteen-wheeler that was halfway across the bridge.

"Looks like a nice day on the river," the box squawked.

"Come on down," Linda said and then added, "Where you headed?"

"Indianapolis, little lady. Want to come?"

Linda smiled. Buddy didn't look too pleased. "She gets calls at home all the time," he said. The boat leaped ahead.

It began to rain harder, and I was glad we were under cover on the powerboat. Mist moved in over the water. We passed under the Burlington-Bristol bridge, and I could just make out the riverside park where my expedition across Burlington County began.

As we charged downriver, a northbound, green speedboat veered in our direction. "Buddy," I said, but he didn't respond. "Buddy!" I said, louder this time. No response. "Here comes that sonovabitch John!" Buddy cried out in glee. Just short of a head-on collision both boats cut and reversed their engines and then rocked in the waves, inches from each other.

"Whadya say, John?" Buddy called out of the cabin window.

"How's it hanging, Buddy?" replied John, who stood in his open boat, the rain running down his face. He held a beer can in one hand while, with the other, he nervously moved the wheel back and forth.

"Pretty fair," Buddy said. "Whatcha doin'?"

"Nothin' much. What are *you* doin'?"

"Oh, just hanging around. Whatcha up to?"

"Just cruisin' up and down the river. Who're those guys on your boat?"

"Coupla fakes. They say they're canoeing to Philadelphia, but me and the old lady's carried them five miles already. So how's it hanging, John?"

"Pretty fair," John said.

The conversational powers of both men seemed to be exhausted, but they stayed alongside bobbing for some moments more until Buddy suddenly said "Let's go" and peeled out like a hot-rodding teenager, his bow high in the air. "Some crazy guy, that John," Buddy said. "He's got a V-8 Chrysler in that thing."

Approaching Buddy and Linda's Northeast Philadelphia boat launch, we faced a crisis. "Do you want to stay here?" Buddy asked, "Or do you want us to take you down to Center City?" It was raining hard now, and the forecast was for more of the same. The daylight was beginning to fade.

"Center City," Phil said, brimming over with good humor. He was into his fourth beer.

"Wait a minute," I said, "this is supposed to be a three-day trip."

"Okay," Phil said. "So we get a hotel room and fool around in Philly for the third day."

"But we're supposed to get to Philadelphia by canoe," I said.

After considerable argument, we compromised: I agreed to a hotel room that night; Phil agreed to finishing the trip on our own power. We would leave the canoe and gear at the boat launch office, ride down to Center City with Buddy, and get a hotel room for the night. In the morning we would come back out again, get the canoe, and paddle the ten miles to downtown.

We pulled the canoe out of the water at the boat launch, but, before we could lift a finger, Buddy had the canoe over his head like some enormous, ceremonial hat and was striding inland toward a big white building. We trailed behind, carrying the paddles and the plastic garbage bags with our gear. As we were returning to his boat, Buddy volunteered to bring us back in the morning. "Not doing anything special," he said.

Buddy took the wheel and opened the boat up. We charged down the Delaware, passing under the Tacony-Palmyra bridge, the Betsy Ross, and a railroad bridge in quick succession. The *Linda* took a glancing blow from something in the water, veered on its side, and righted itself. Buddy drove on without comment. Lord, I thought. What if that was one of the ties I'd used to test the Assunpink tunnel?

Phil asked Buddy how long he'd had his boat. "About two weeks," Buddy replied. "Traded in my Winnebago."

Ahead we could just make out the blue outline of the Ben Franklin Bridge through the rain. Passing under it, Buddy maneuvered the boat against the Market Street pier, the very place where Benjamin Franklin arrived for the first time in Philadelphia at the age of seventeen. Phil and I climbed out and scaled the wall. "Bye," Linda said.

"Call me in the morning," Buddy yelled as he gunned the boat upriver.

Walking up the pier, we passed through a break in the wire fence and out into the lights of the now dark city. I felt stiff and strange. Shy even. I was sure everyone in the streets knew that the great urban canoers had sneaked into Philadelphia the night before their scheduled arrival. But it was also delicious to be secretly looking for a hotel when we were supposed to be in a tent and to be enjoying the city without the burden of an automobile or suitcases, with just a few dollars and one credit card in our pockets.

We walked into hotel after hotel, but had the same bad luck I'd had on my walk across Philadelphia. Worse: this was Sunday night of a holiday weekend; all the hotels were full, even the Apollo. A policeman mentioned the Hamilton Inn, and we phoned them from a booth on Chestnut Street. They had one room left, actually a suite. We hailed a taxi and raced to the hotel.

The Hamilton Inn had seen better days. The bald desk clerk was either deaf or was not listening. The elevator man, who sat tilted back against the wall, appeared to be asleep. But the suite was well worth the eighty-nine dollars we paid for it. The bedrooms were enormous, with fourteen-foot ceilings. The sitting room had fat, acid-green armchairs and sofas and real oil paintings on the walls. The suite looked like someone had sealed the door in 1930 and no one had entered it since. The elevator man told us President Hoover once stayed in this suite. He didn't tell us he also died in it.

While I was in the shower, Phil made a phone call. I could see him through the tattered shower curtain and open bathroom door and wondered who he was talking to. He didn't say anything about it when we went out for Chinese food nor after returning to the suite, where we watched an old Japanese horror movie. "That's you," Phil said, panting. "The creature from the black lagoon."

Midway through the movie, there was a knock on the door. Who could be knocking on our door in the Hamilton Inn in downtown Philadelphia?

Phil's girlfriend Abigail, that's who. The bastard had phoned Abigail, and she had driven down to Philadelphia to spend the night with him. Abigail was to have picked us up in Philadelphia at the end of the trip, but Phil had invited her down the night before. Abigail is an interior decorator. She took a professional look around our suite and said, "Funky."

Soon Abigail and Phil departed for Phil's room, and I was left watching the movie by myself. When it ended I repaired to my room and lay there staring at the ceiling and wishing I too was lying next to something soft. Didn't every hardworking urban adventurer deserve such a reward? Why hadn't I been smart, like Phil, and called Patricia and proposed a conjugal visit?

My envy dissipated the next morning. At breakfast in the hotel coffee shop Phil and Abigail were having a fight. She wanted to come along for the last day's paddle on the Delaware, and Phil kept telling her that the canoe would be too tippy with her sitting in the middle.

Abigail said something about "male bonding."

"Why's everyone so hot to put down male bonding?" Phil replied. A couple of guys get together to have a canoe trip and all of a sudden it's *male bonding*."

"You think women are only good for one thing, Phillip," Abigail retorted.

"Just because I don't want to tip over the canoe I think women are only good for one thing?" Phil rejoined. His learning came in handy now. Phil invoked the names of real and fictional heroine adventurers such as Amelia Earhart and Sissy Hankshaw, the great hitchhiker in Tom Robbins's novel *Even Cowgirls Get the Blues*. He trotted out the film *Thelma and Louise*.

Abigail was having none of it. "Fuck you, Phillip," she said. "And fuck you too, Michael," she said, turning to me. "You're a pair of macho assholes." Then she stormed out of the coffee shop.

Phil looked down at the mouth. "Pussy-whipped," he sighed. I wasn't sure whether he was complaining or simply describing the state of affairs.

Earlier in the conversation, before the fight started, Abigail had mentioned spending the day at the Philadelphia Art Museum. Would she be there when we got back to Philadelphia? If not, how were we getting home?

I phoned Buddy from the pay phone in the hotel lobby. He said he would be by for us at 10:30. Phil and I bought a couple of newspapers and stood under the hotel marquee reading.

Buddy showed up five minutes early. He said Linda was still sleeping. We got into his Cadillac and headed for I-95 North. A fine rain was falling. Off to our right we could see the Delaware through the mist.

By 11:15 we were out on the water. The tide was with us, which almost made up for the rain. Phil had on an army surplus khaki slicker, but all I had was a windbreaker, which, London Fog or not, was not waterproof. An oil barge escorted by two tugs moved laboriously upriver. It was so slow that we forgot to pay attention to its wake; it caught us broadside and broke right across my lap. I was left with an uncomfortably soaked crotch to go with the generally damp rest of me.

A sailing regatta overtook us, passing silently downriver in single file like a flock of giant white birds. All the sailors wore proper yellow foul-weather gear and Docksider shoes, and there were lots of pale, rimless glasses and pipes in evidence. I felt pretty scruffy next to these water aristocrats.

We were, nevertheless, making great time. One by one we reached the bridges we had sped under the evening before with Buddy and Linda. The river got wider as we moved closer to the ocean, and there were more boats and they were bigger.

The river took a bend. Far downstream I could just make out, through the mist, the jagged Philadelphia skyline and the crackerbox buildings of the Campbell Soup Company across the river in Camden. However much we had cheated with tows, meals on the town, and sleeping in the city, we were going to make it to Philadelphia by water.

As we got closer to the Ben Franklin Bridge, we began looking for a place where we could get the canoe out of the water and into the streets beyond. There were high walls at every pier, and some of them had fences as well, including the Market Street pier, where Buddy had dropped us the night before.

Just beyond the bridge was a pier with an orange, white, and blue police boat moored alongside. A policeman eyed us suspiciously, but he grabbed our bow rope and helped pull us onto the pier. He said we could leave the canoe there for an hour while we went looking for Abigail.

Soaking wet, we took a taxi to the Art Museum and mounted the broad staircase made famous by the *Rocky* movies. There was a bronze statue of the actor, Sylvester Stallone, in prize-fighter togs on top of the steps. I hear they've taken it away since, though it apparently attracted, during its brief residence, much interest among multitudes who ordinarily avoid museums.

Abigail was in the room with the Thomas Eakins collection. We approached her sheepishly, but she seemed to have forgotten the fight. "Did you know," she said, pointing to a portrait of Walt Whitman, "that Eakins took the ferry from Philadelphia across to Camden every day to paint this picture, and Whitman, who was living there then, always asked him, 'What's the weather like on the Delaware?' He was very old then, dying, but he always asked Eakins about the river—the waves, the wind, the tides."

"Right," Phil said, gathering courage. Water pooled on the stone floor around both of his sneakers; he looked half-drowned. "So aren't you going to ask *us*?"

"Ask you what?" Abigail said.

Abigail had parked Phil's station wagon on the Benjamin Franklin Parkway. We went down the museum steps, drove to the police pier, and loaded the canoe atop the roof rack. Then we headed back toward New Jersey, Abigail going on about Eakins and Whitman, Phil silent all the while.

I was silent, too, deep in my own thoughts. I found myself thinking of Henry David Thoreau and wondering what he would have thought of the Philadelphia water adventure and of the other adventures as well. Thoreau built his cabin on Walden Pond to get out of town, while in all of my adventures I had striven to get *into* town. Like other Americans I have always revered Thoreau's isolated cabin of a century and a half ago. But what, Henry, I wanted to ask, have you done for us lately?

In his essay "Walking," Thoreau wrote, "Eastward I go only by force; but westward I go free." I had gone eastward in my adventures, but not by force, by choice. Unlike Thoreau and Huck and Jim and Daniel Boone I hadn't gone with the flow; I had willfully gone against the current of American history and life.

For I had wanted powerfully to do things no one had done before, to traverse a new frontier, and I felt now as if I had done a bit of this in my adventures. I felt peaceful. I had made it back to that hillside above Interstate 287 after all.

There was, however, a small conflict in my thoughts. I was eager to see Patricia and the children and tell them about the Philadelphia trip. But after struggling with the filthy Assunpink and insane boys and the terrors, however imaginary, of the tunnel and Ralph's betrayal and our rejection at Pennsbury and the tides in the Delaware and the near crash with Buddy's friend

John and the compromise of ideals when we stayed in a hotel and the tension with Abigail and the anxiety over whether she would be there at the end to get us home and traveling to Philadelphia not once but twice—by canoe, powerboat, and car—it seemed not only anticlimactic but unjust that it was going to take only one uneventful hour in Phil's station wagon to get home.

About the Author

Michael Aaron Rockland is professor and chair of the American Studies Department of Rutgers University. Earlier, he had a career in the United States diplomatic service. *Snowshoeing through Sewers* is his seventh book.